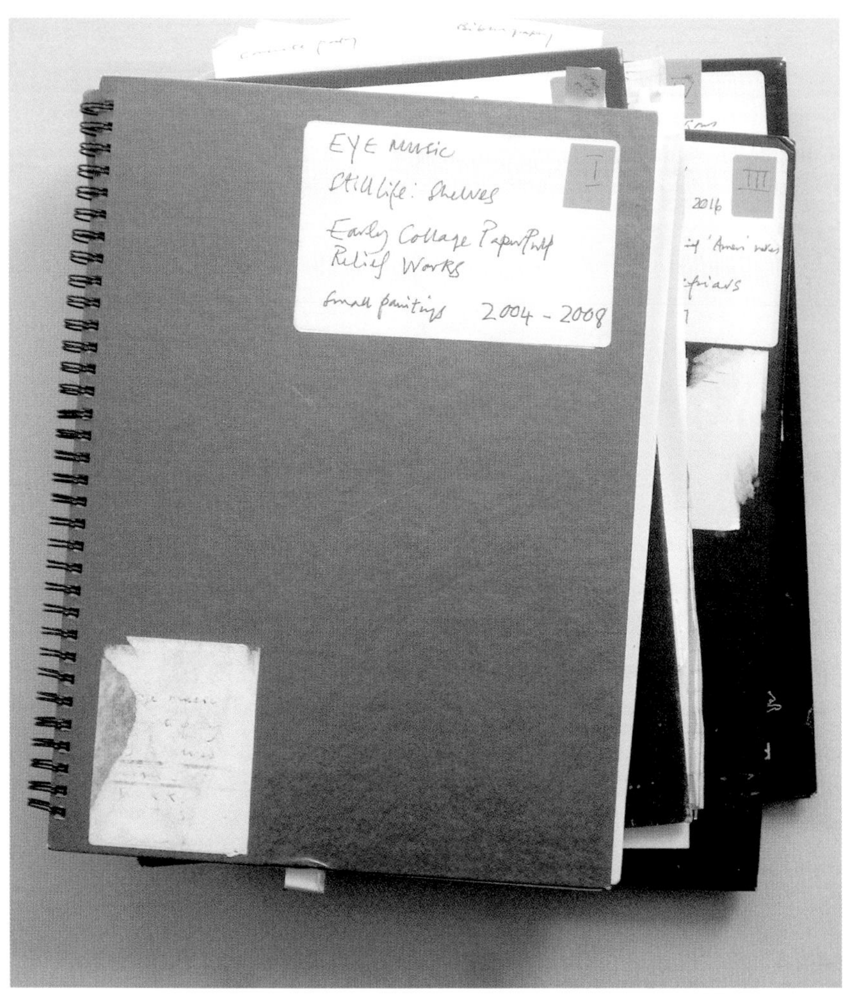

'Eye Music' notebooks I–IV, 2004–19

Janet Boulton

Eye Music
Series & Performance

Uniformbooks

First published 2022
Copyright © Janet Boulton
All rights reserved
ISBN 978-1-910010-33-4

Photographs: Janet Boulton, Peter Finnegan, Tim Fransen, Hugh Palmer
Image archive: Tim Fransen
Text editing: John Bevis, Richard Mortimer

Uniformbooks
7 Hillhead Terrace, Axminster, Devon EX13 5JL
uniformbooks.co.uk

Trade distribution in the UK by Central Books
centralbooks.com

Printed and bound by T J Books, Padstow, Cornwall

"One day I must be able to improvise freely on
the keyboard of colours: the row of watercolours
in my paintbox."
—Paul Klee, *Painting Music*

"Matisse has taught the eye to hear."
—Riva Castleman, *Henri Matisse: Jazz*

Contents

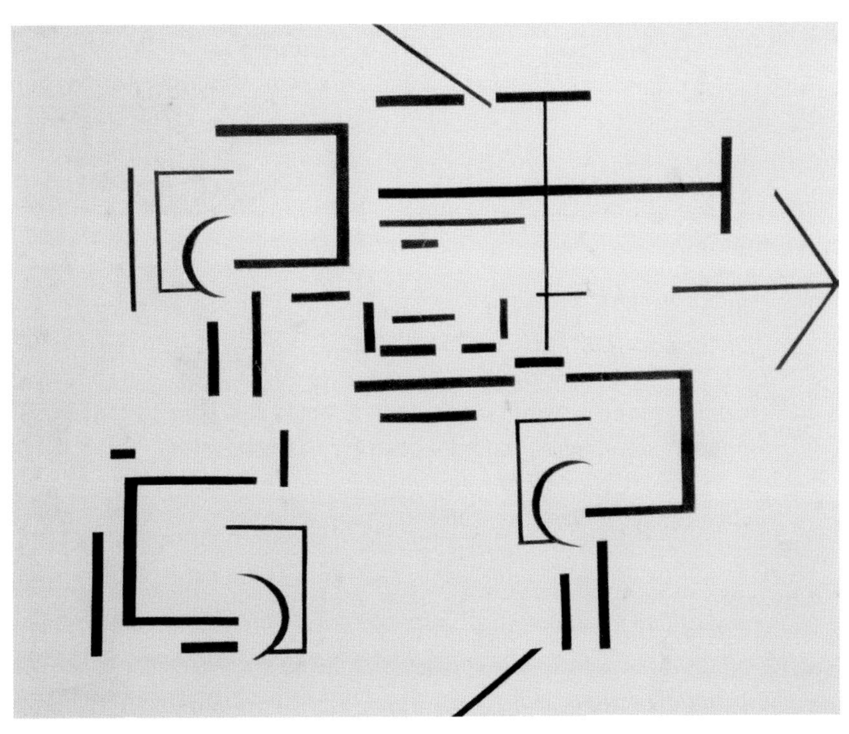

1. *Generating Station, Diagram I*, 1960

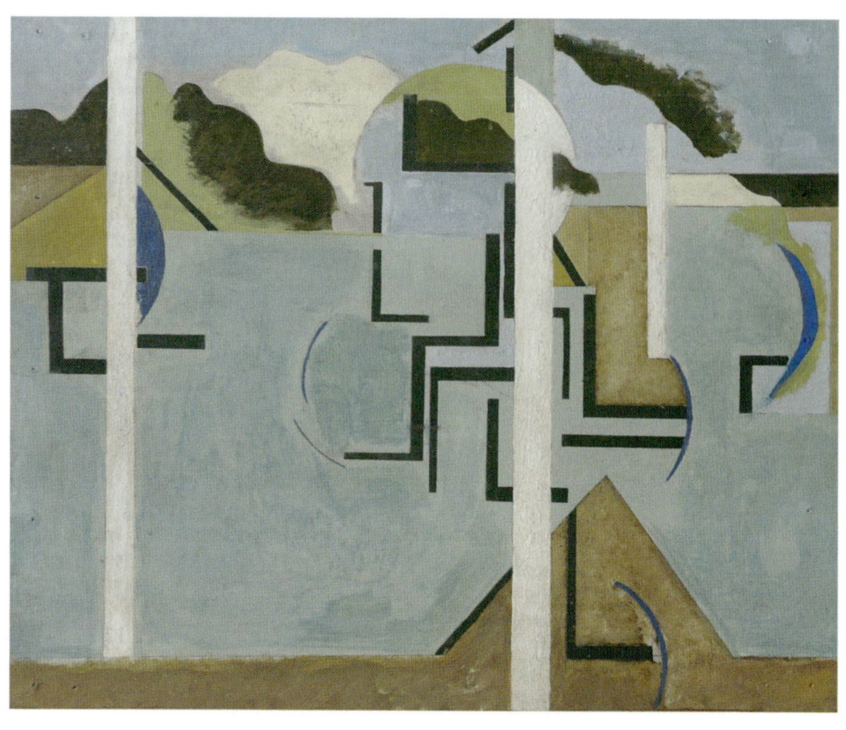

2. *Generating Station in Landscape*, 1960

Preamble

As so often when tracing the beginnings of ideas I find myself in our village church attending Sunday School or being in the choir. Hymns and psalms were sung to the sound of an organ, while following the musical notation in an old leather-bound hymnal.

At school, many classes were greatly enlivened by the illustrations in the pages of what were mostly dry old books. For instance, geography texts incorporated plenty of maps, geological diagrams and weather charts, which were made up from a variety of fascinating marks, whose patterns, lines and shapes were diligently copied into exercise books to illuminate, indeed cheer up, a boring essay. I relished the novelty of the pale blue-squared graph paper, a tiny mapping pen and the glossy Indian ink.

Mathematics lessons, everlastingly a mystery, were almost entirely redeemed by the beauty of geometry and its specialist equipment: the protractor, set square, compasses, and a carefully sharpened pencil. Similarly, within the dark labyrinths of arithmetic and algebra, most of the time the best that could be done was to make a neat arrangement of the elegant abstract signs and symbols to be found amongst all the numbers and theorems.

During piano lessons, a highpoint of the year was being given the new music required for the next examination. On opening the book for the first time, reading the title, and seeing the shapes of the notation rising and falling effortlessly among the horizontal staves, the light and dark notes, curves and parallel lines. The manuscript as a whole, with its foreign words and arabic numerals, seemed a graceful expressive thing in its own right, without the necessity of being realized in sound.

Thus, in the course of everyday life, we absorb of the existence of other non-verbal means of communicating and are introduced to the wider world of semiotics.

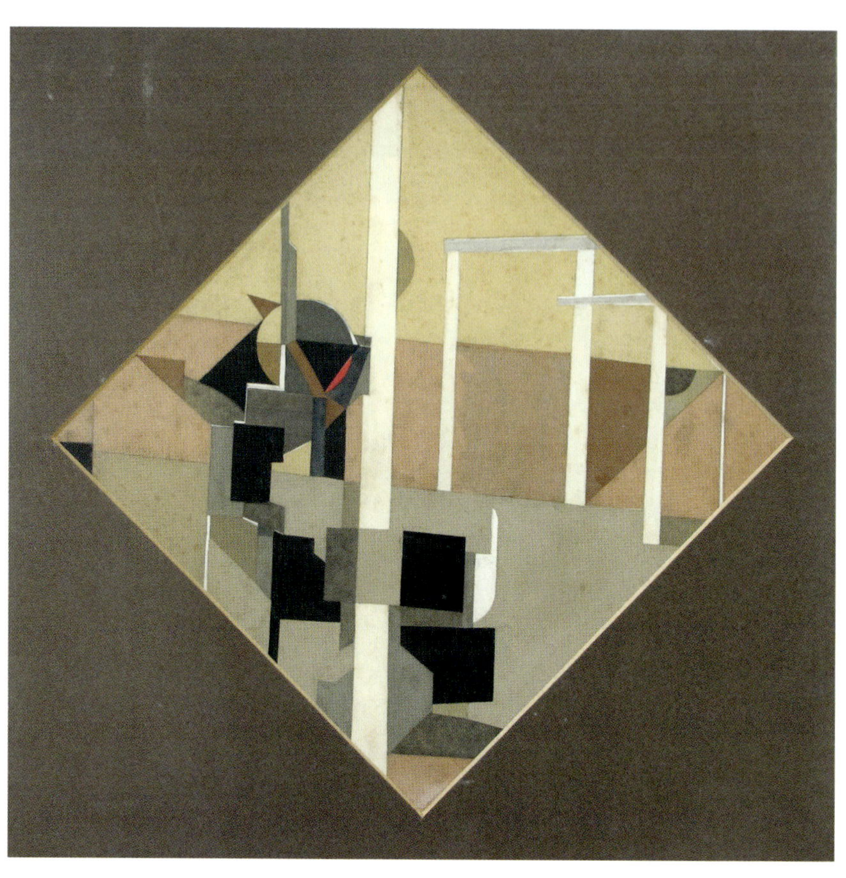

3. Generating Station, January, 1961

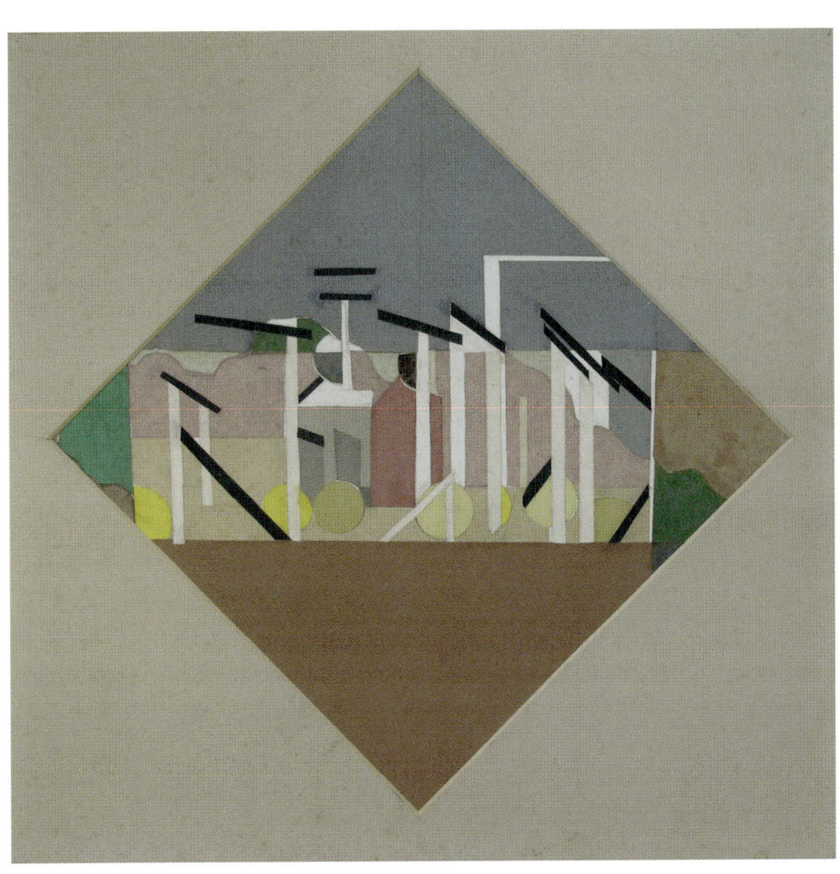

4. Generating Station, Spring, 1961

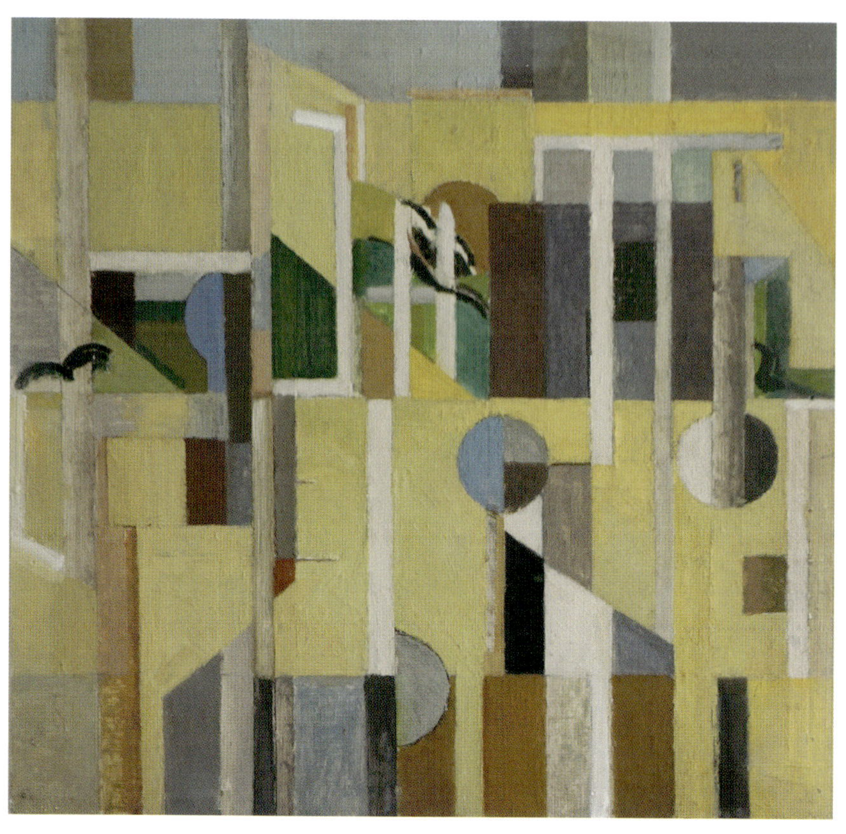

5. *Generating Station with Concrete Posts*, 1961
6. *Generating Station, Diagram II*, 1961 / 7. *View of Generating Station*, 1961

12

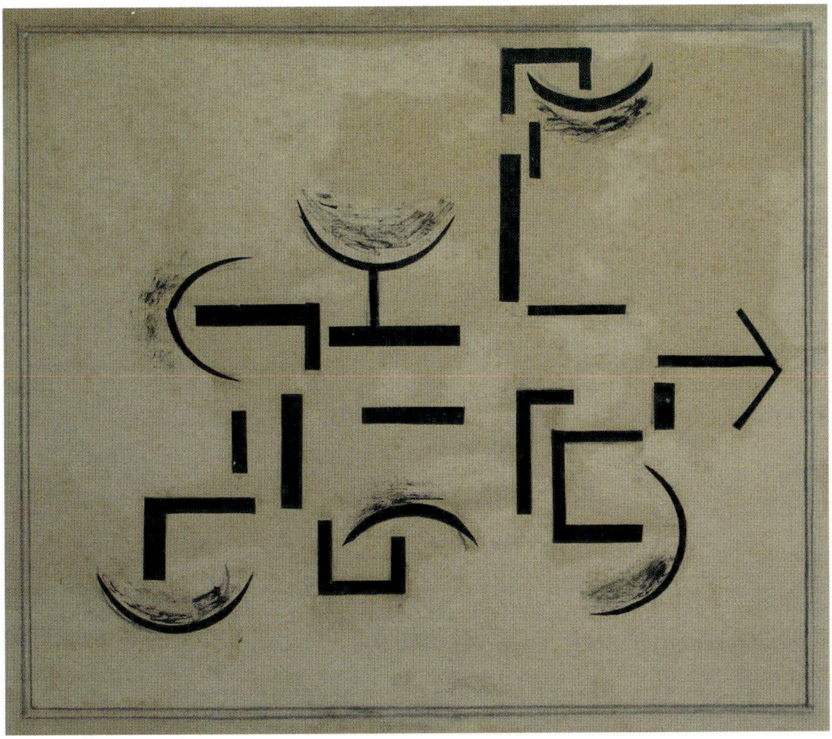

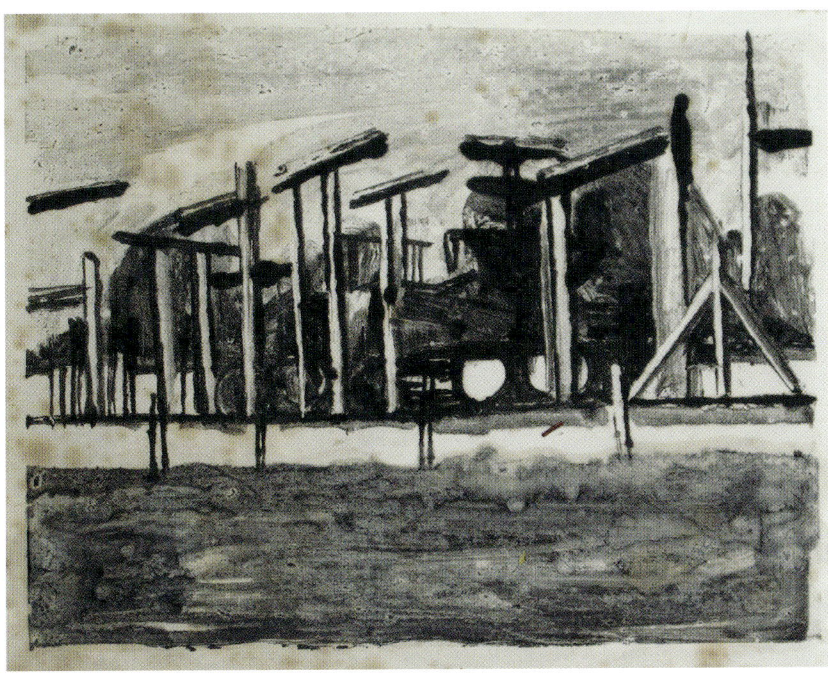

Still Life

The still life, shown here, is representative of a life-long fascination with glass and its potential as a subject for painting, particularly as seen in windows and mirrors, with all their many spacial and reflective possibilities. It was only in the early nineteen-eighties that my interest began to extend to the ordinary glassware to be found in abundance on the shelves of most charity shops. It was the functional inexpensive everyday jugs, bowls, cakestands, jam jars, pyrex plates, paste pots, and tumblers that I collected.

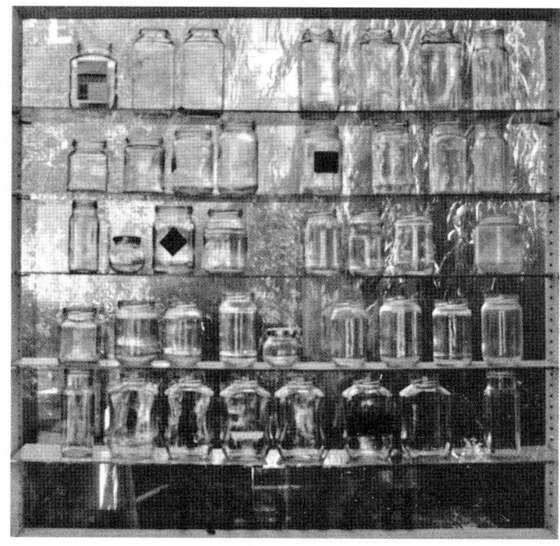

This particular still life, set in the studio window, was installed thirty years ago and celebrates the common jam jar. I like spending time arranging things. It was put in place as much to enjoy—as a presence in its own right —as for a future subject.

On occasion, over the years, it has been altered by re-assembling the configuration of the jars and their labelling, but the basic structure within the window and the position of the plate glass shelves has remained untouched, except for some periodic dusting. Observing the ever-changing light, tone and colour going on in the garden outside, has the effect of keeping the whole arrangement current and alive.

It was in 2004, over twenty years later, that a start was made on this series of paintings and paper relief works. In the tenth century St Bernard of Clairvaux said, "Hearing leads to sight". Conversely, in these 'Eye Music' pictures it could be said "Sight led to hearing", since the long process that led to making them came, initially, through considering the purely visual possibilities of the still life in the window.

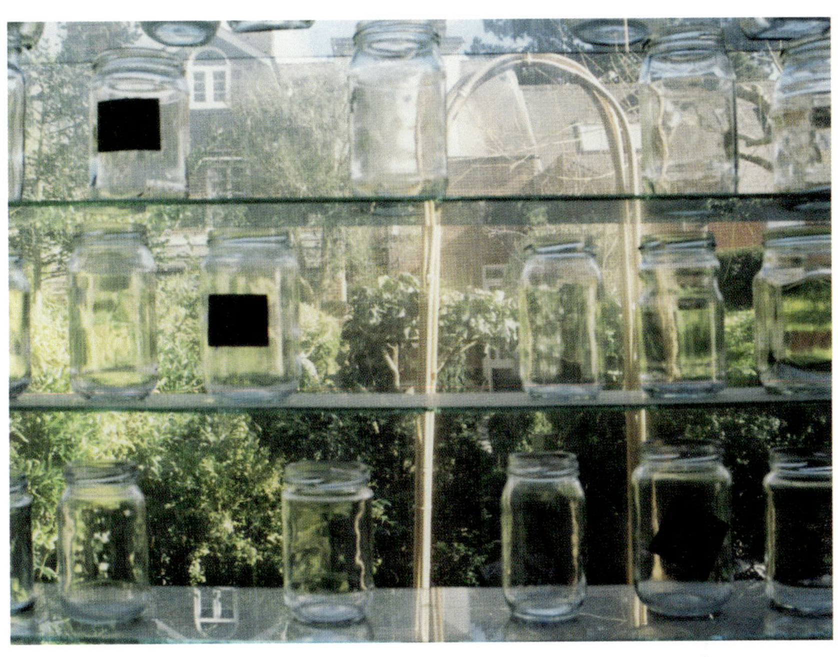

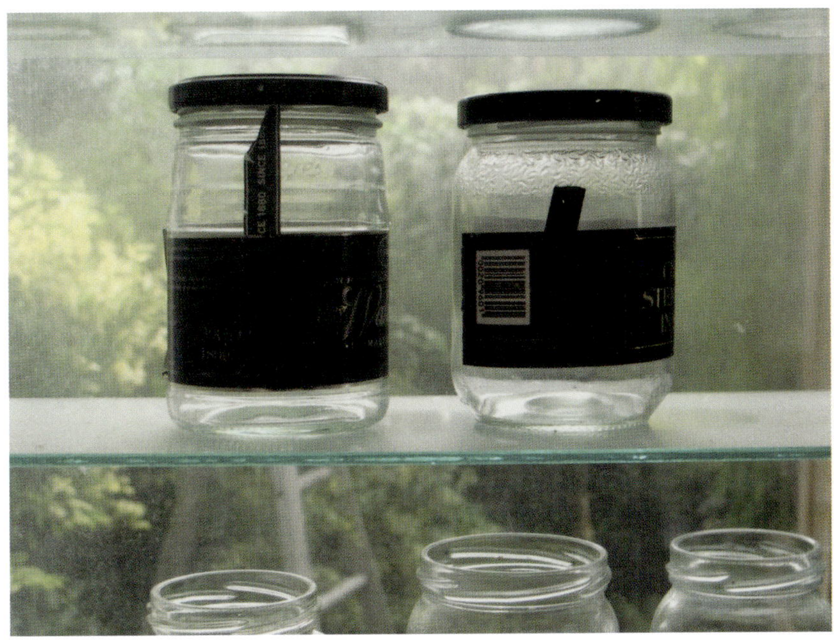

Jam jars, glass shelves, studio window, 2022

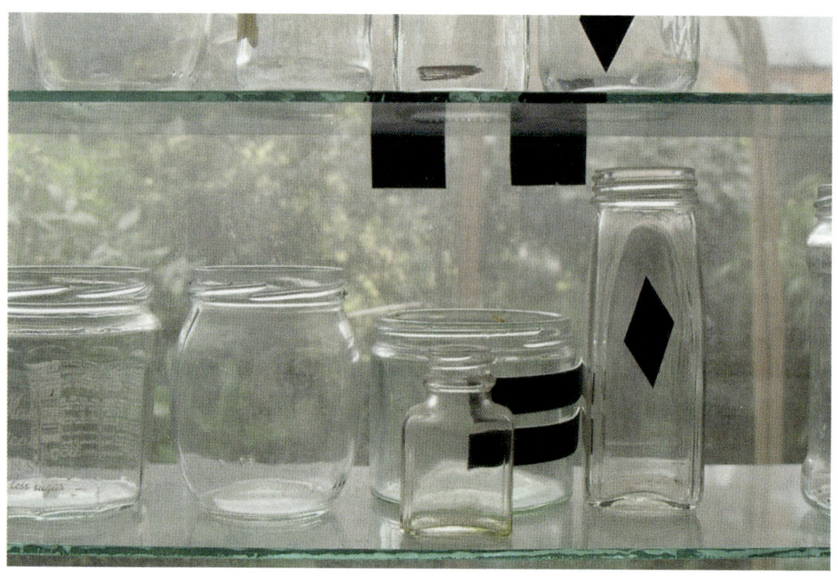

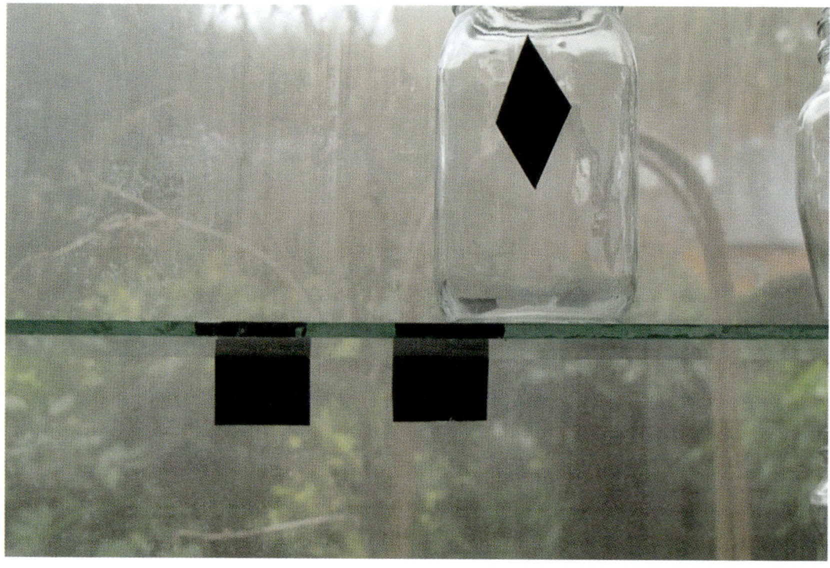

Jam jars, glass shelves, studio window, 2022

Jam Jar

The jam jar has a number of attributes. Being a simple cylinder made up of vertical, horizontal and elliptical elements it contains the all-important 'cube, cone and sphere' defined by Paul Cézanne as fundamental in his researches into the universal nature of form.

The label represents, to me, a connection with those early twentieth-century followers of Cézanne—the Cubist painters Braque, Picasso and Gris. These artists incorporated many graphic devices along with the naming of people and things in common usage into their still life pictures: for instance, "Vin" on a bottle of wine or "J. S. Bach" on a sheet of music beside a violin, or the name of a loved-one.

Thinking further along these lines, I eventually (whilst attending the Holy Week celebration of the Tenebrae at Blackfriars in Oxford) saw a connection between the jar with its label and the early medieval musical notation used for plainchant:

> This form of musical notation… was widely used from the eleventh to the thirteenth century. By making a direct connection between the words and the music it became easier for the singers to keep a steady and serene sound, no matter how difficult or dissonant the combinations of certain syllables.[*]

The idea of strong black squares, rectangles and lozenges, grouped within the framework of verticals (the window) and horizontal staves (the shelves) seemed to reinforce and substantiate the musical content of the pictures, giving me a wider, more relevant

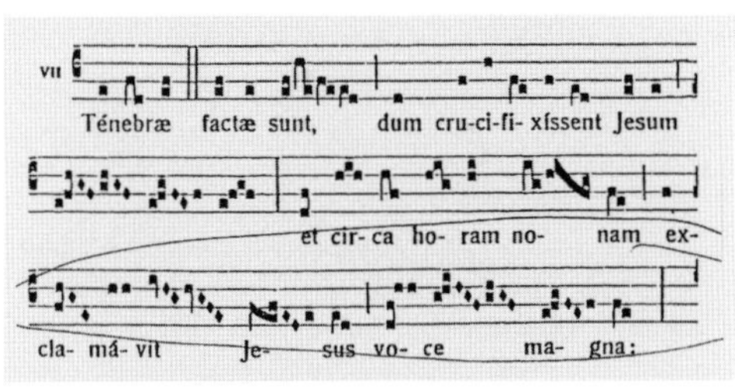

vocabulary. Gardner Read's work contains lists of the classical accentuation signs amongst which was a table of simple neumes (grk. *neuma*: sign/nod). They were all comprised of straight lines depicting rising and falling inflections—diagonals, parallels, formations of dotted lines, zig-zags etc. with expressive names, which, translated from the Latin were 'rod', 'dot', 'point', 'little stroke', 'bend', 'climber', 'twisted', 'extended'.

[*] Gardner Read, *Music Notation: A Manual of Modern Practice* (Victor Gollancz, 1974)

Construction

Another discovery, early on, was finding that when making the support to contain the still life, it inadvertently formed a construction which bore similarities to the pages of a conventional musical manuscript. Namely, the five plate glass horizontal shelves enclosed in parallel vertical lines with a shallow perspective.

This basic shape gave me a regular and standardised format on which to base all the works in this 'Eye Music' series. Added to which, the static and rather flat, repetitous nature of the glass still life arrangement is offset, indeed liberated, by the contrasting freedom and movement inherent in the view of the garden as well as to be found in musical composition. Moreover, by appropriating the simple graphic shapes of early musical notation I gained the tools and the language whereby, in a process of deconstruction and re-invention, I could make pictures which embraced the formal and random languages of both painterly and musical traditions and ideas. It is as if an abstract occurence is taking place in a real space.

The idea that colour and musical notes are intrinsically related has been in existence since Isaac Newton split the optical spectrum into seven colours and linked them to the seven notes of the musical scale. Since that time there have been innumerable important treatises and theories about the relation of colours to sound and emotion as well as to each other. In twentieth-century European painting, artists such as Kandinsky, Kupka, Klee, van Doesburg, and Itten all turned to colour theory alongside musical values as prime sources in their researches into abstraction.

The choice and the arrangement of the colour, the tones and the graphic elements in this series of paintings and relief works is purely subjective, being personal and random. The pictures are neither a blueprint nor a musical score. They are not prescriptive of any instrumentation or performance and have no starting or ending point—but they do have music in mind.

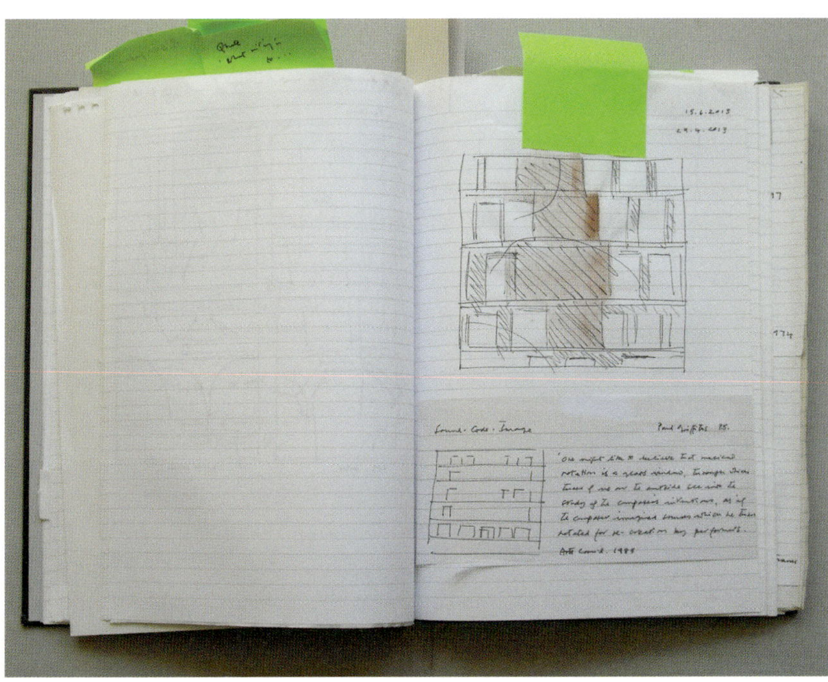

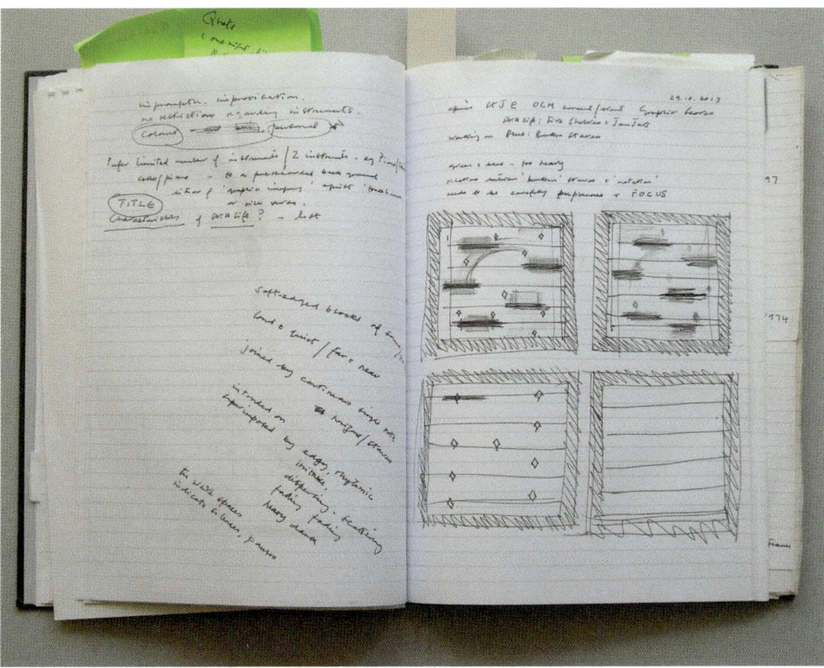

'Eye Music' notebook II, 2004–13

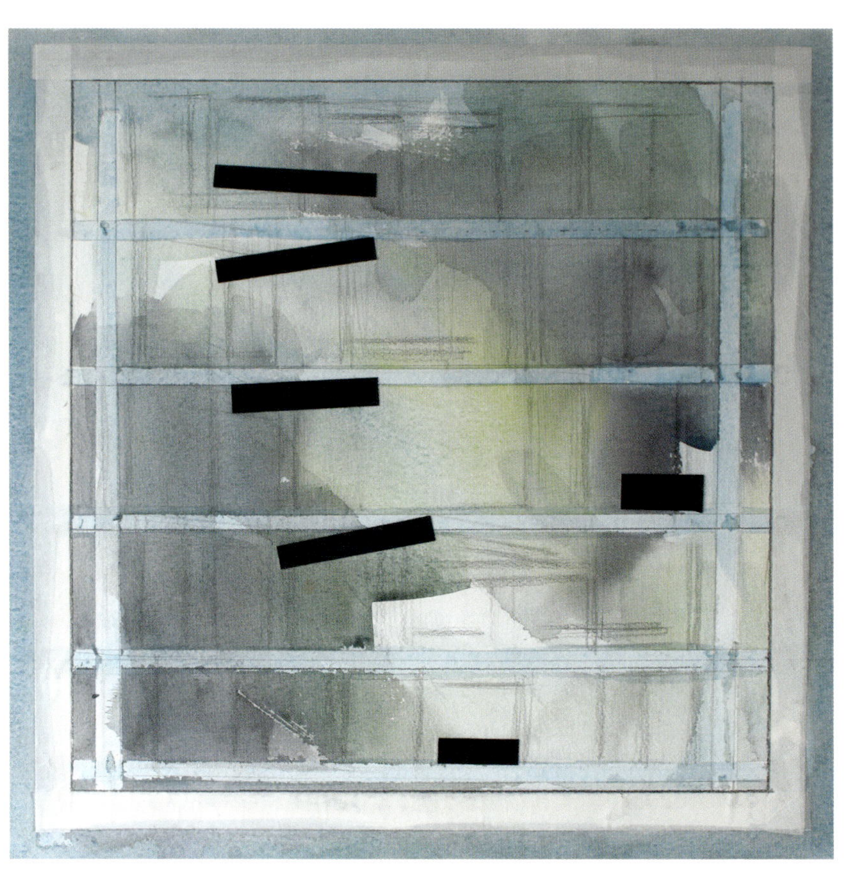

8. *Early Study I*, 2004

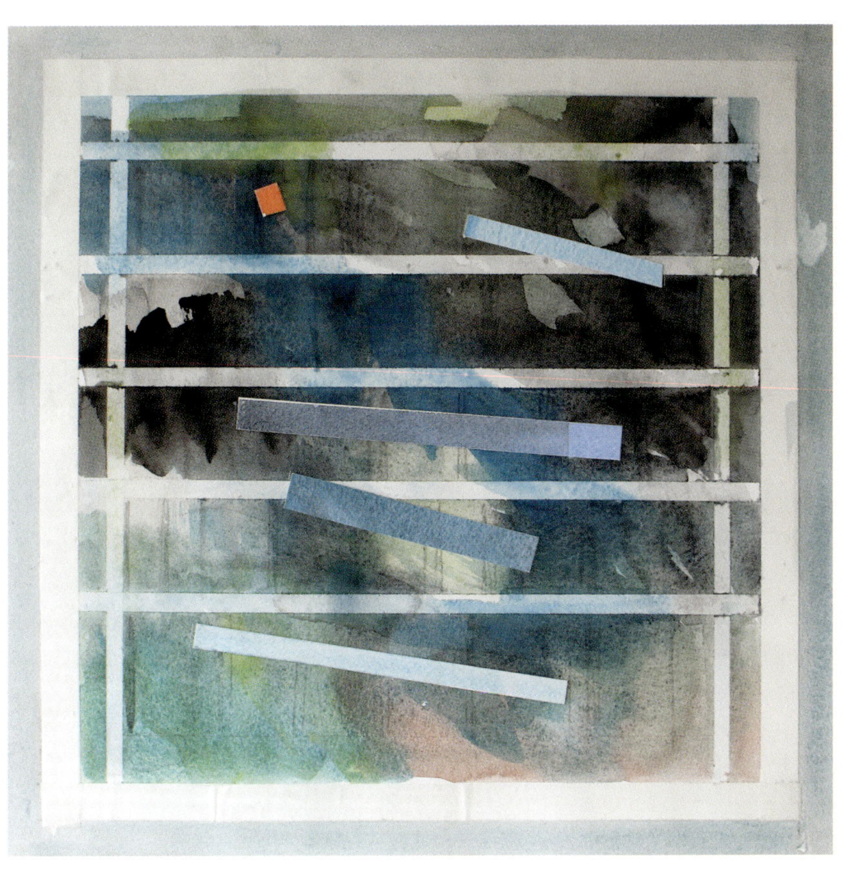

9. *Early Study II*, 2004

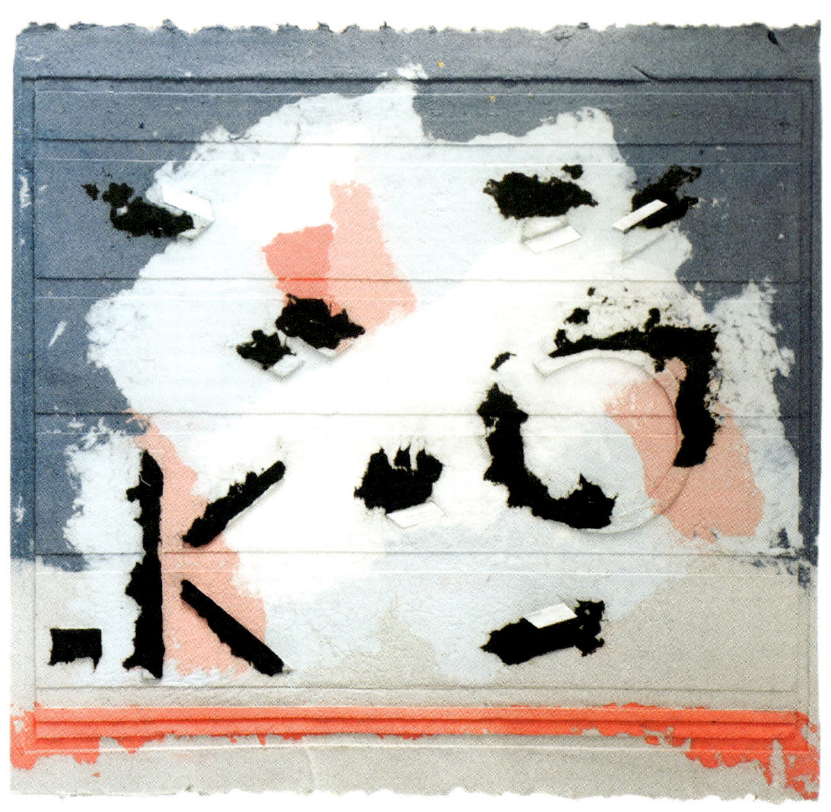

10. *Early Music I*, 2005

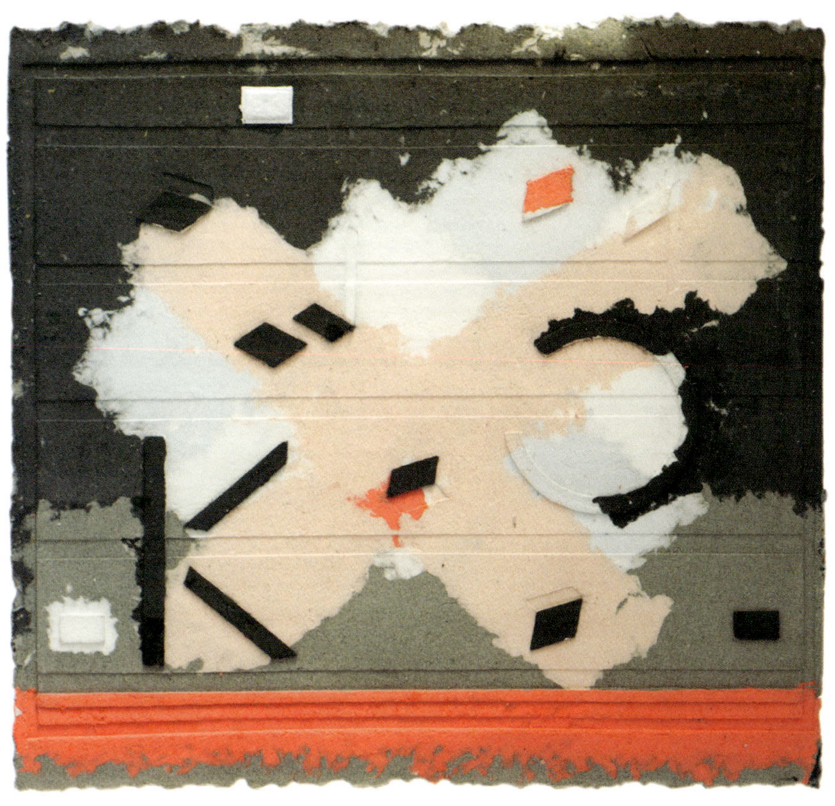

11. *Early Music II*, 2005

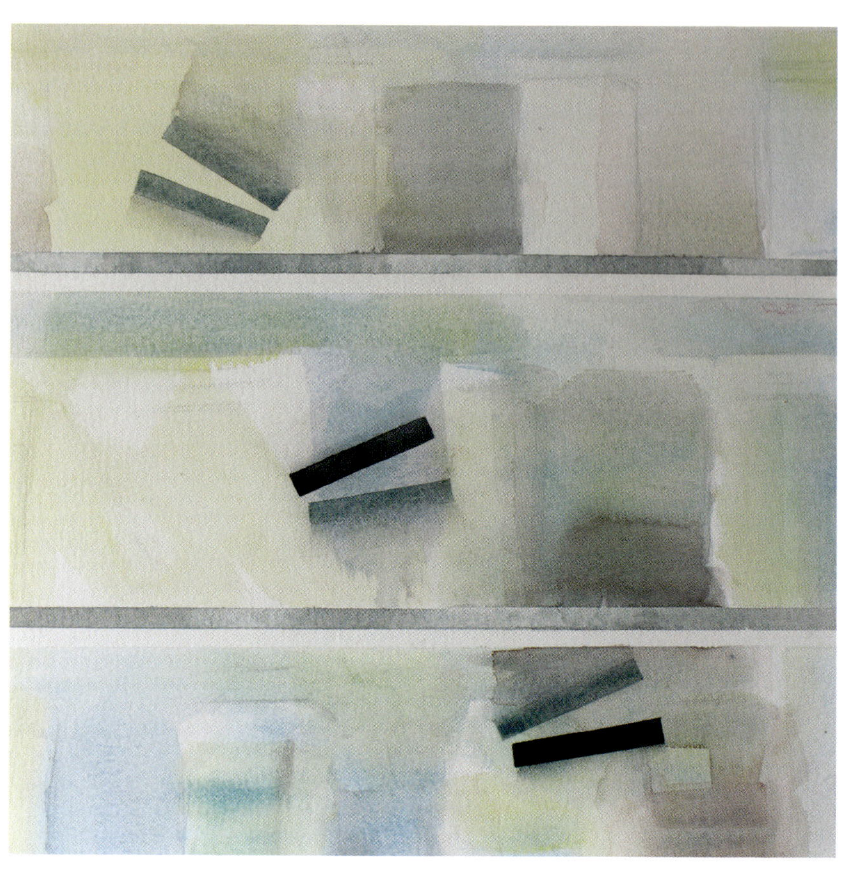

12. *Jam Jars in a Window*, 2005

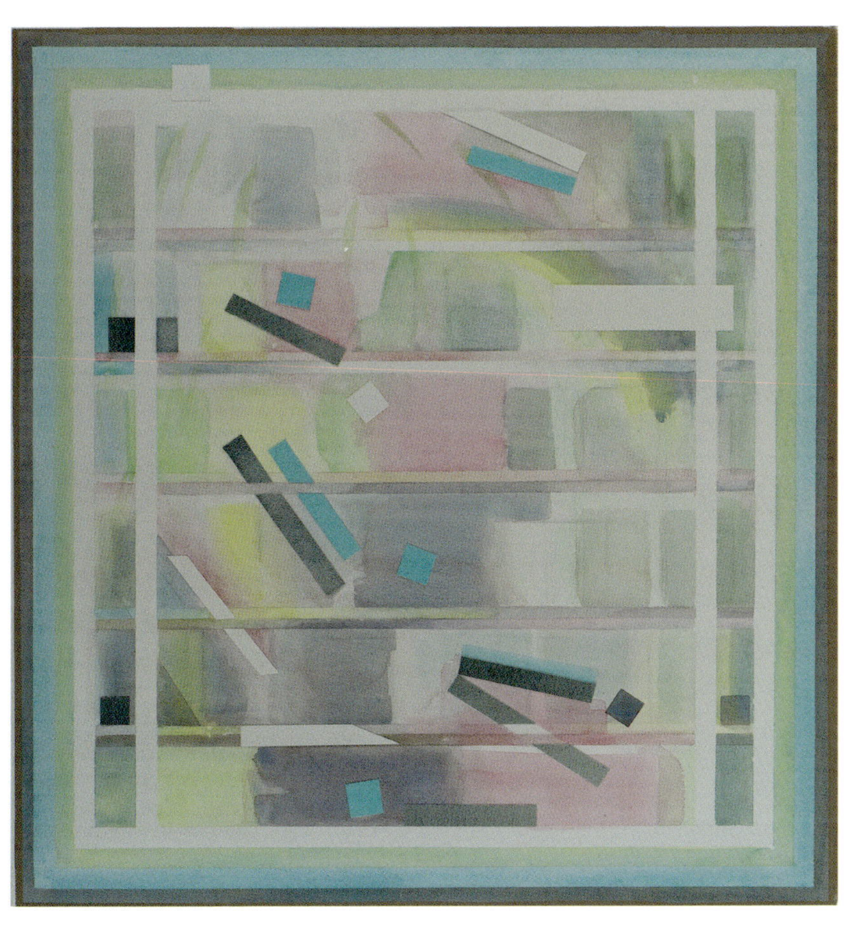

13. *Jam Jars in a Window, Pink & Turquoise*, 2006–11

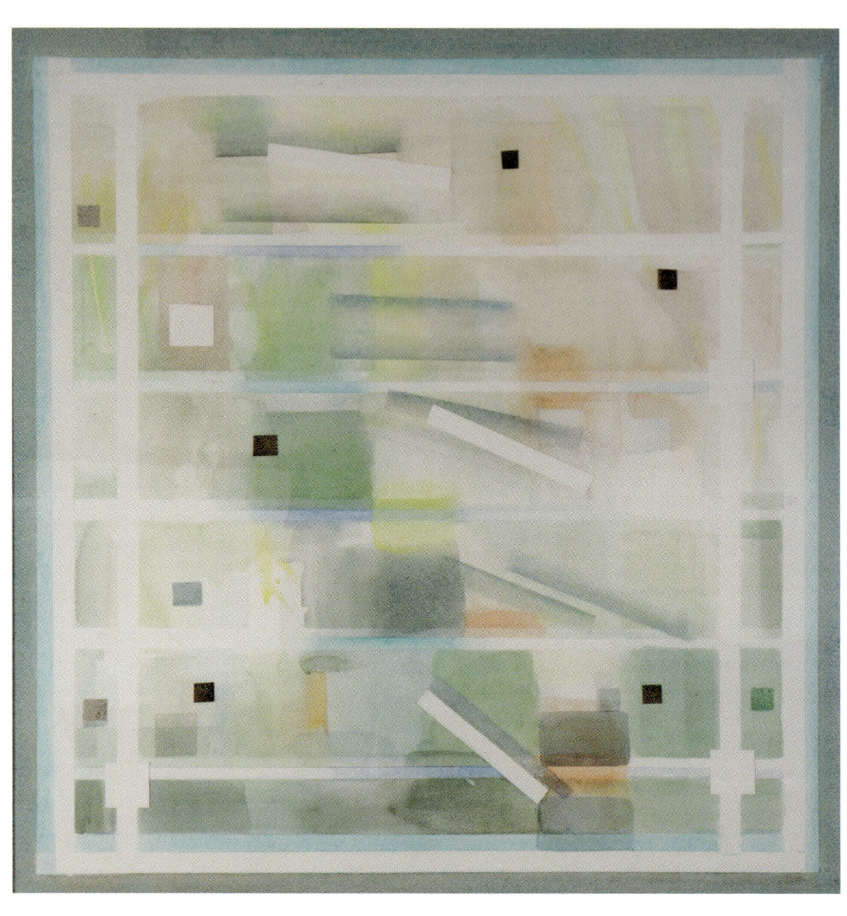

14. *Jam Jars in a Window, Green & Terracotta*, 2006–14

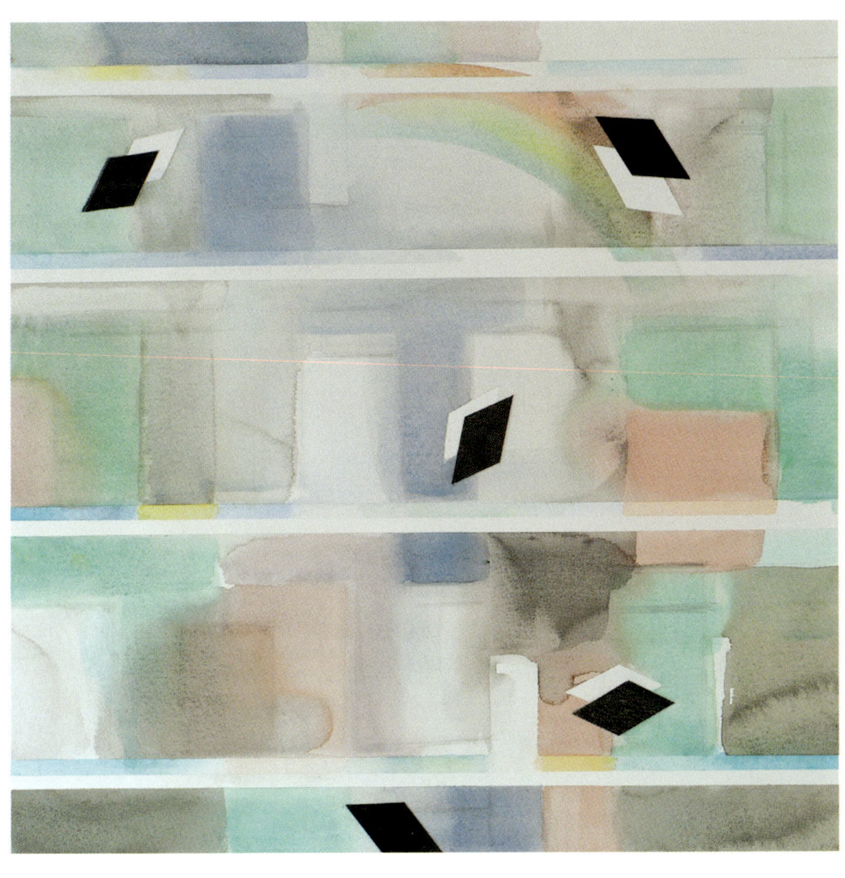

15. *Jam Jars in a Window, Green & Terracotta*, 2011

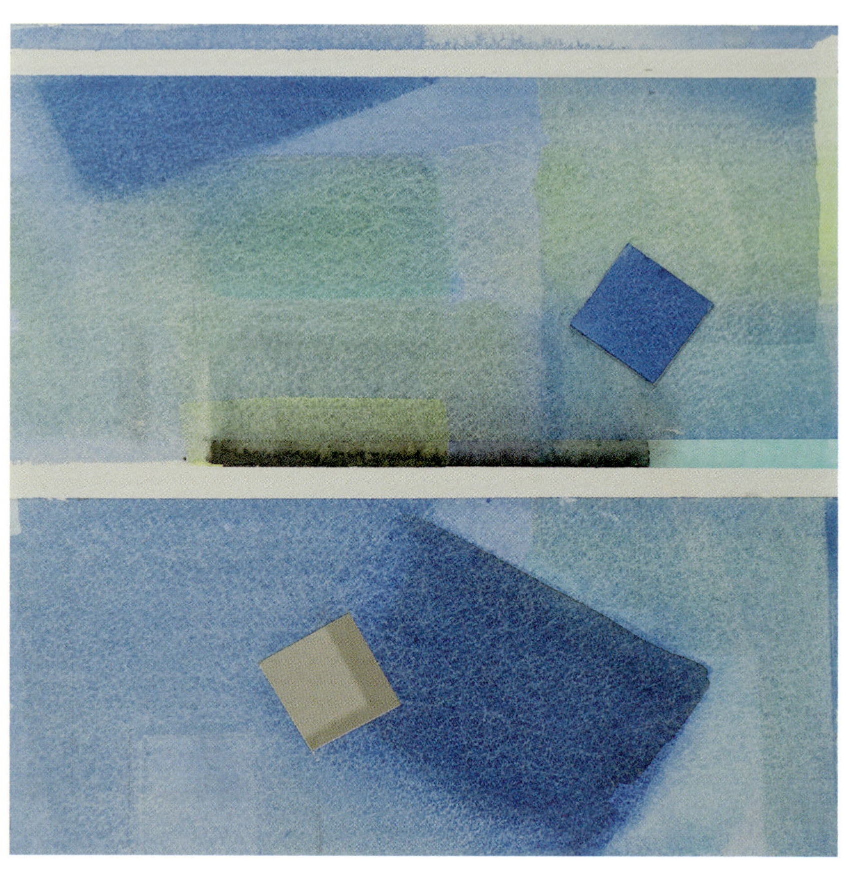

16. *Study I, Blue & Green*, 2011

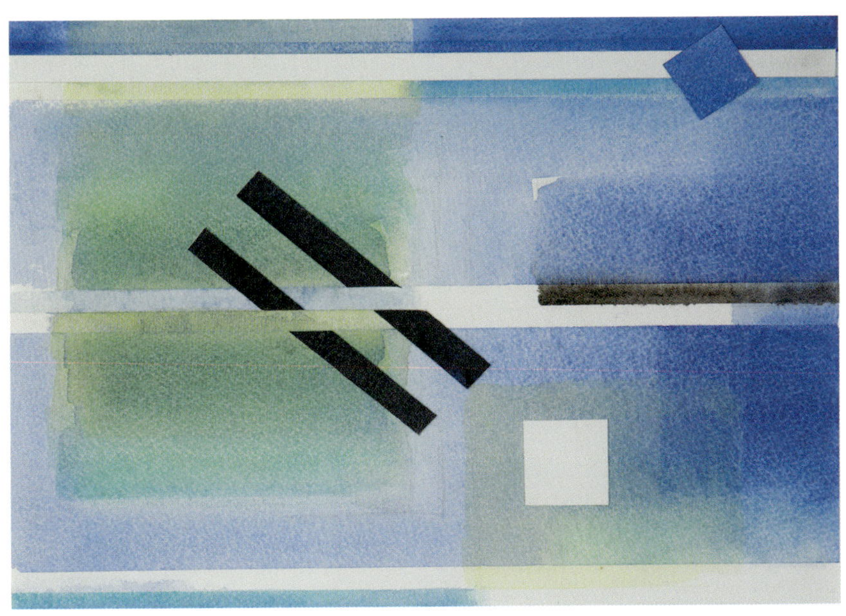

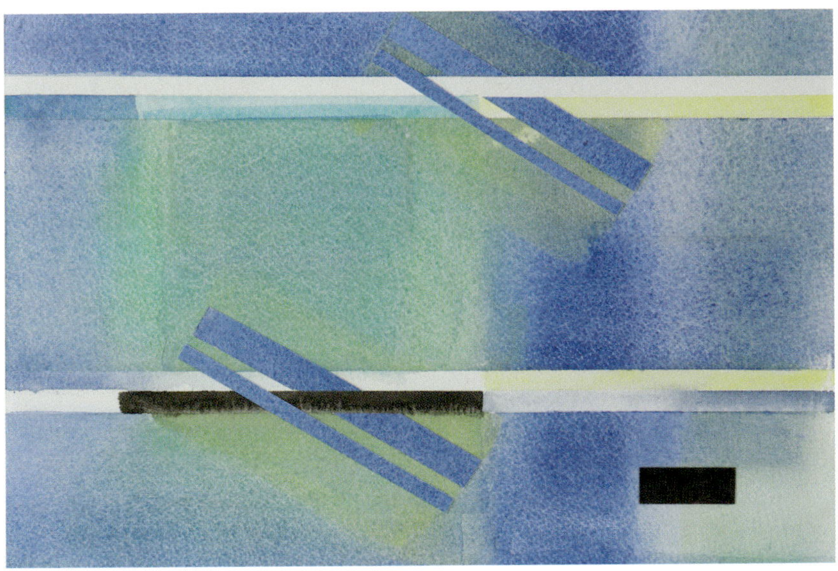

17. *Study V, Blue & Green*, 2014 / 18. *Study VII, Blue & Green*, 2014

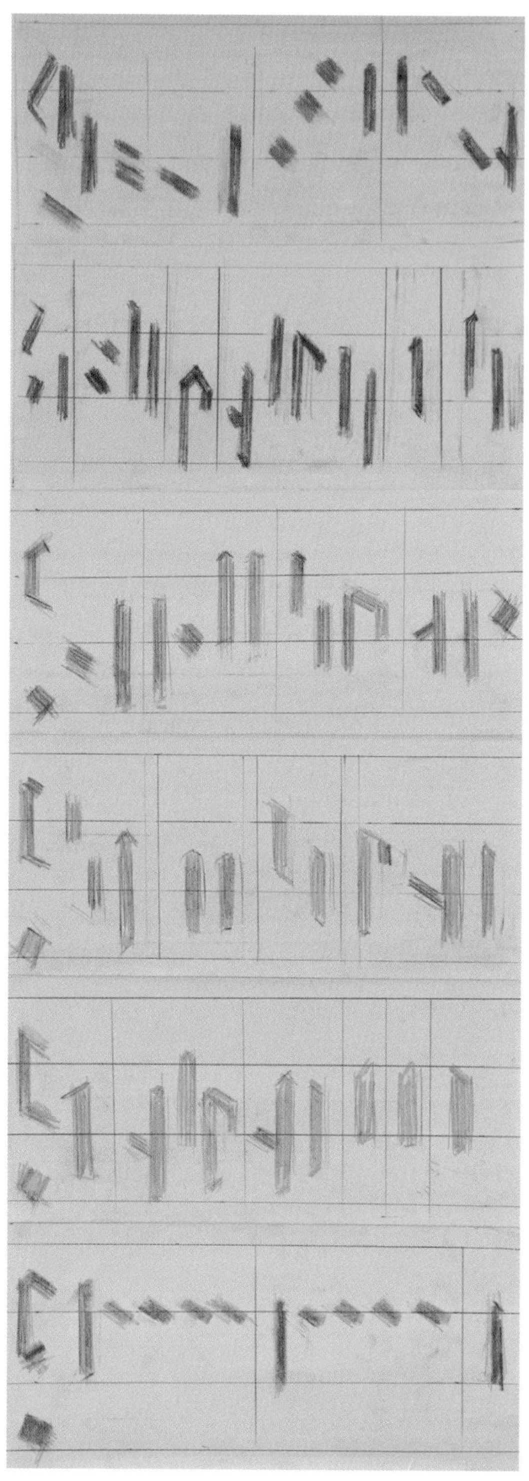

19. *Drawn Scores*, 2013

Keble College Library, Oxford

In 2004 the composer, Simon Whalley, came to see the first paintings I had made in the 'Eye Music' series. We discussed the possibility of an event—which would combine an exhibition with staging musical performances in response to the pictures.

However, it wasn't until 2010 that I could resume work on the series. In the spring of 2013 he came again and saw the new developments which included not only the watercolours but also a number of paper-pulp reliefs related to the subject. In his role as Director of Music at Keble College, we resumed our conversation about arranging a collaborative event/events, this time, within the college environment.

As a result of this connection I was introduced to the College Librarian, Yvonne Murphy. Since my strongest musical inspiration is from early church music I had a growing wish to look at, and make drawings from, an original early manuscript, rather than seeing illustrations in a history book on the subject. The Library at Keble contains a fine collection of illuminated manuscripts and missals. I was shown six large printed missals originating from a number of medieval monasteries in Europe, some pages of which contained within the main liturgy, areas of musical notation underwritten in script with the related Latin text. It was from these books that I was given permission to spend two days drawing 'below stairs' in the library.

In an attempt to replicate as closely as possible the calligraphic style of the musical notation (and because in that carefully controlled environment there were necessary limitations placed on the use of materials—no pots of water!) I used a carpenter's pencil with its wide rectangular-shaped graphite and small sheets of textured watercolour paper in the hope of getting an insight into the spirit and character, the liveliness and individualism of this manner of notation. At the same time, while turning over the much-thumbed heavy pages, it was possible to conjure up images of the places where these books were used. The candlelight, the rich tones and colours of the architecture, the nuns and monks in their choir stalls, for whom these books were central to worship—a normal part of everyday life.

It was directly from these drawings, made in the summer of 2013, that the relief works evolved and, with their red, white and black colours, became in some way another kind of score awaiting interpretation.

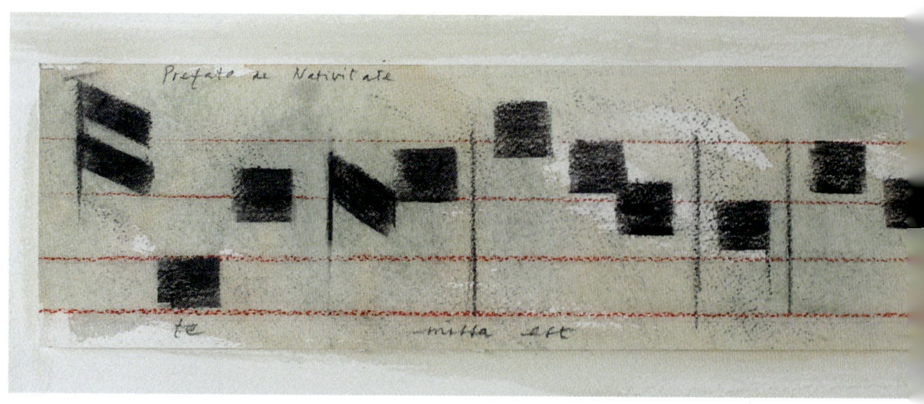

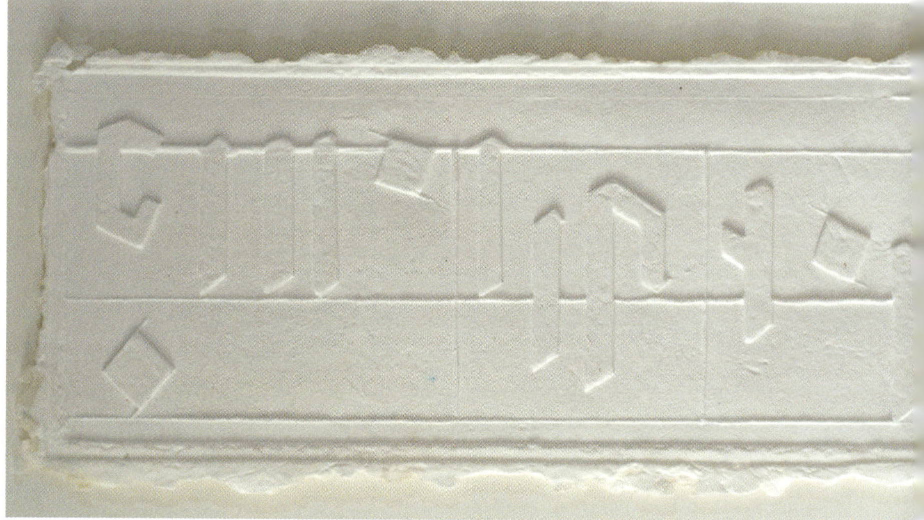

20. *Early Music*, 2013 / 21. *Untitled*, 2013
22. *Red Missale I, 1514*, 2013

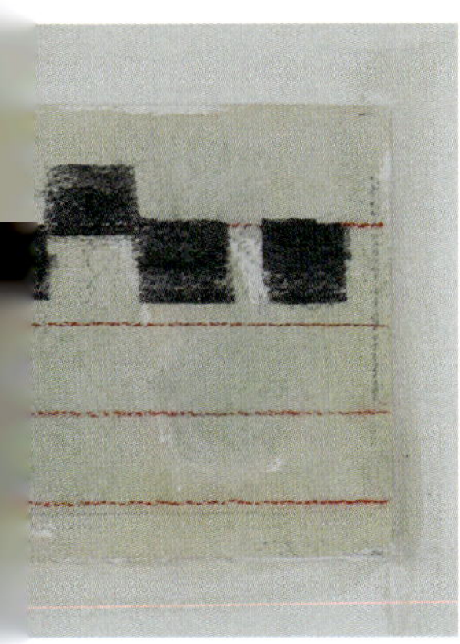

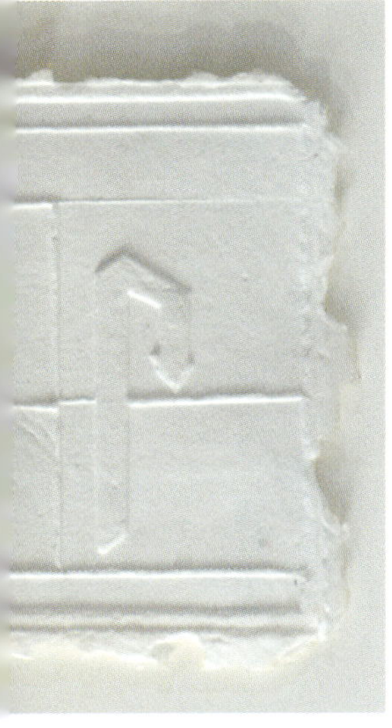

Blackfriars Priory, Oxford

Following the association made between the disposition of jam jars on glass shelving in the studio window and musical scores, it was the participation some twelve years later in the Maunday Thursday service for Tenebrae at Blackfriars Priory during Holy Week in 2016 and the accompanying musical responsories which prompted a deeper interest in the graphic notation of plainchant.

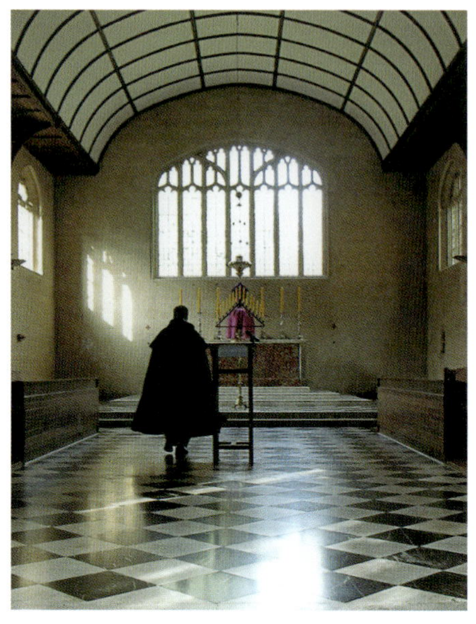

Alongside the musical and liturgical responses, an enactment takes place expressing the gradual reduction of light towards darkness as the last of the candles are extinguished. At this final point the friars, enshrouded in black vestments, dramatically, and in unison, prostrate themselves on the black and white marble floor of the church. The powerful impact of this action is amplified by the simplicity of the uncluttered space of the choir and sanctuary, allowing the emphasis on the symbolic aspect of darkness to be expressed in a particularly direct way.

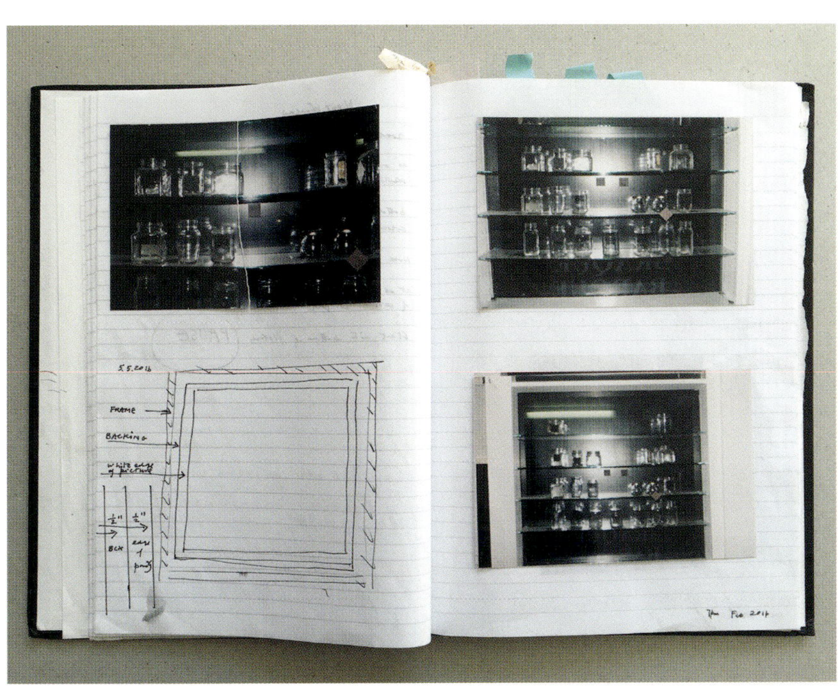

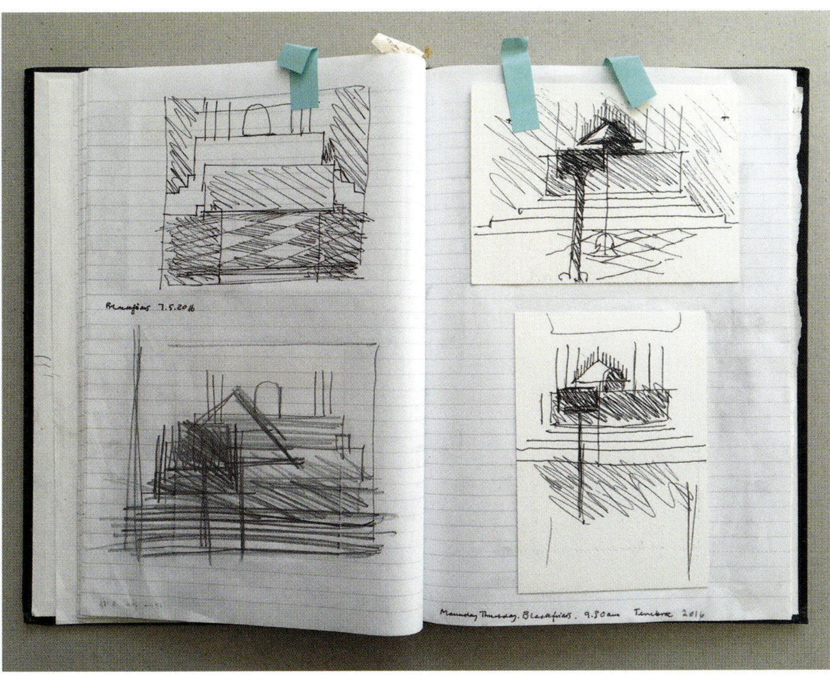

'Eye Music' notebook III, 2016–17

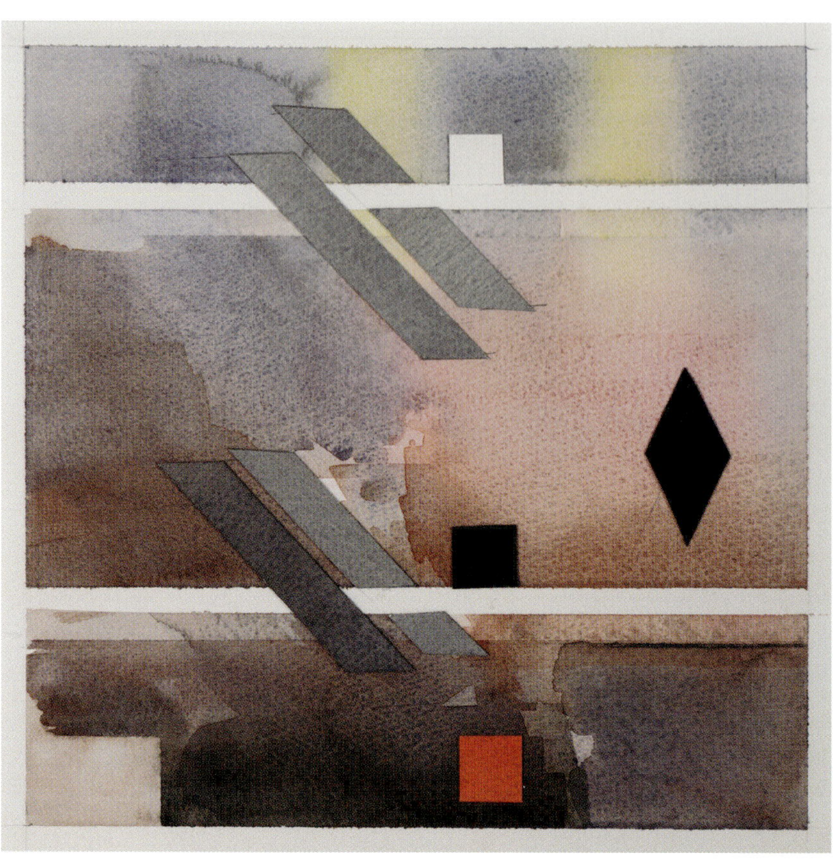

23. *Tenebrae II*, 2016

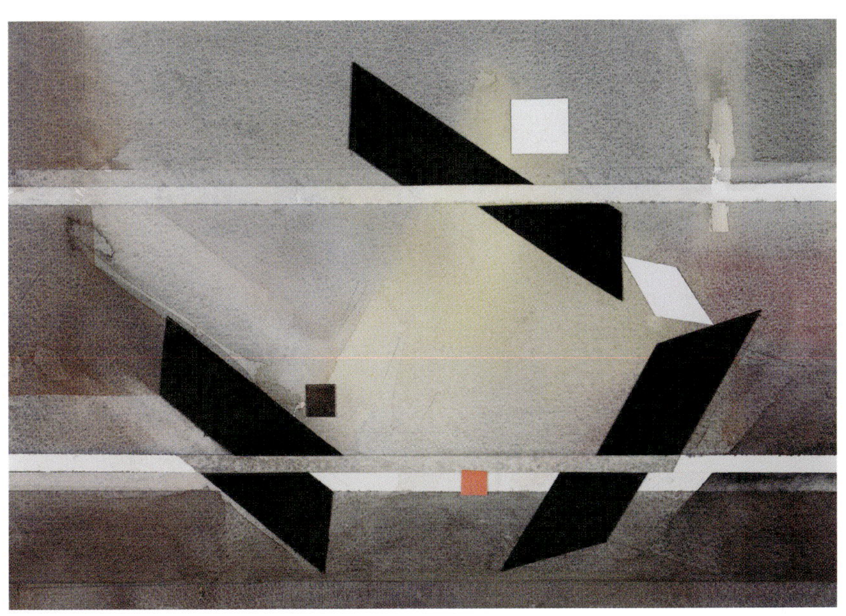

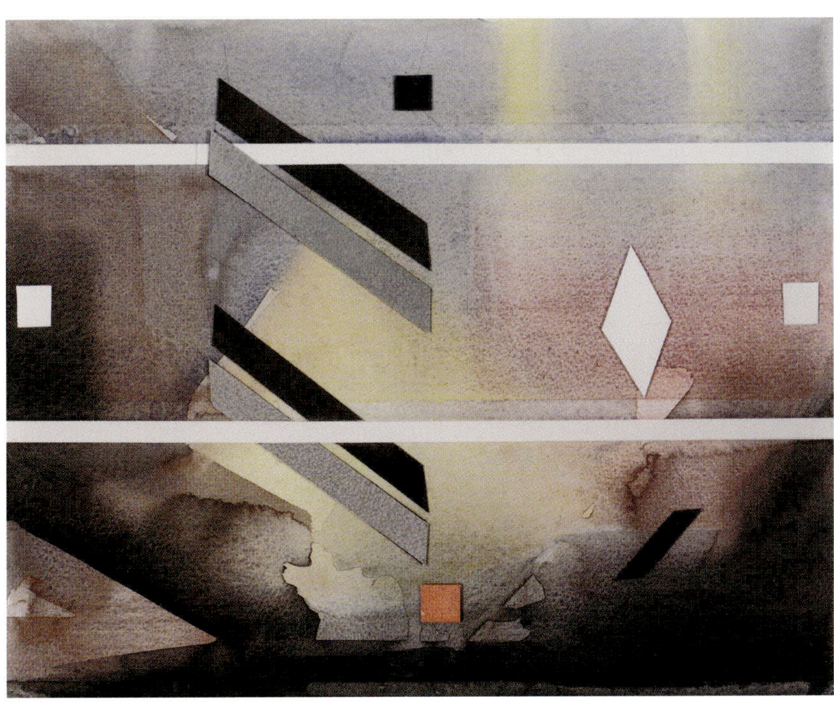

24. *Tenebrae III*, 2016 / 25. *Tenebrae IV*, 2016

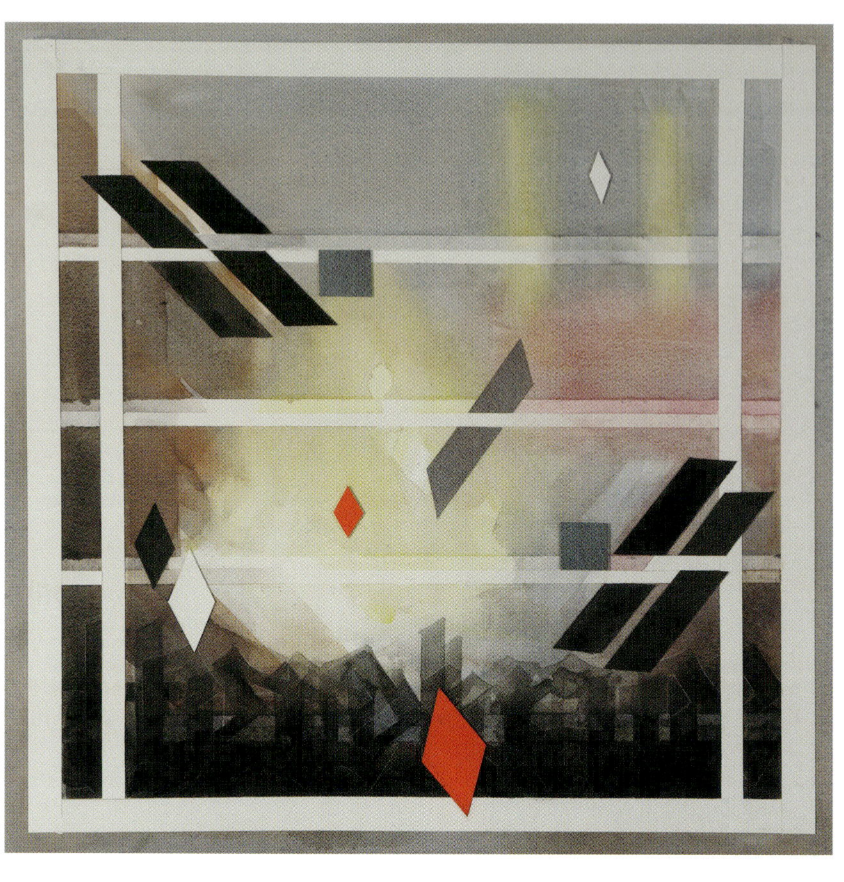

26. *Tenebrae*, 2017

38

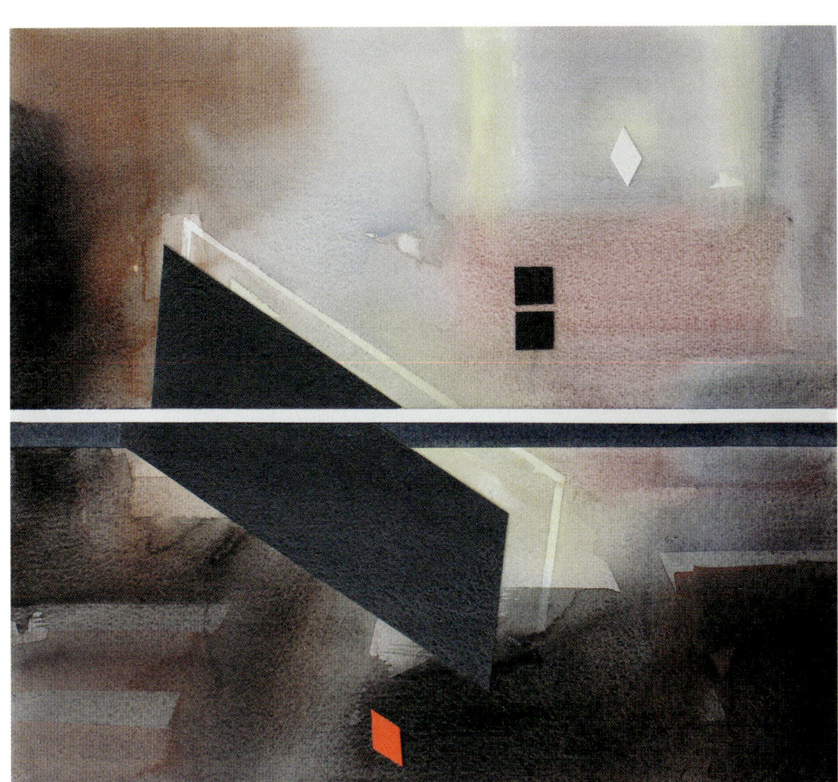

27. *Tenebrae V*, 2018

Merton College Chapel, Oxford

The first performance of Gabriel Jackson's choral composition *Stabat Mater* was in Merton College Chapel at Easter 2018. The east window in the chapel contains fragments of early medieval glass, including a small panel showing Christ on the Cross. Lower down there is a more recent image thought to be of St Frideswide, the Patron Saint of Oxford, but also with her blue robes and downward-looking demeanour reminiscent of the archetypal depiction of Mary, Mother of Jesus. These most iconic images, in the context of the chapel choir and high altar, are reconfigured and associated with the expressiveness of Jackson's contemporary musical notation.

The four bars (opposite) were chosen because of the appearance of the musical notation and the meaning of the related text: *"luxta crucem…"*. The rich variety of shapes and forms with their linear, graphic and flowery characteristics, along with four rocking cradle-like cadences, seem to encapsulate on the page a purely visual expression of grief, and the highs and lows of this poignant and powerful subject.

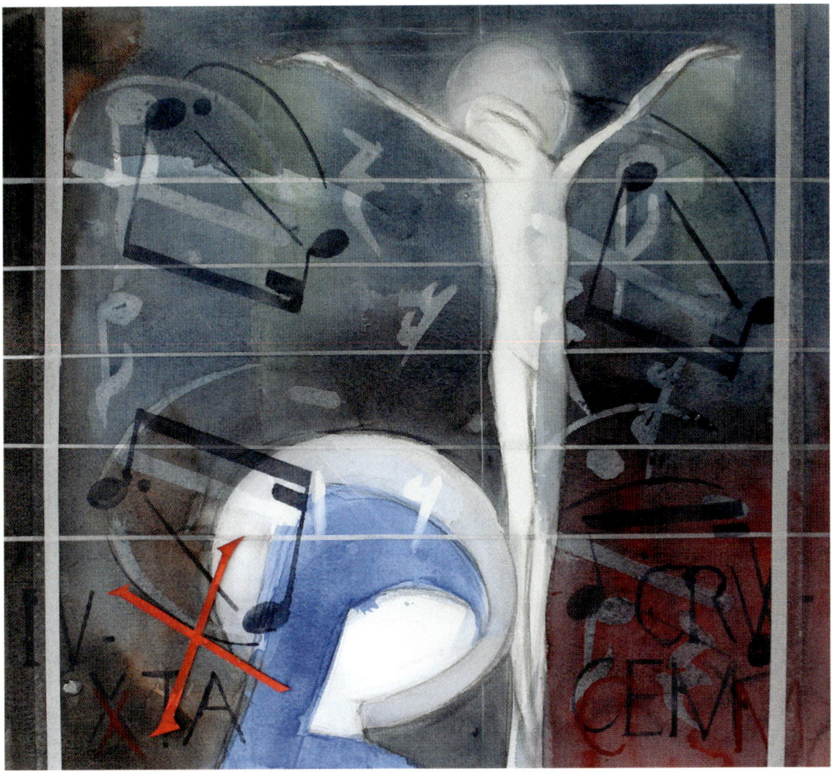

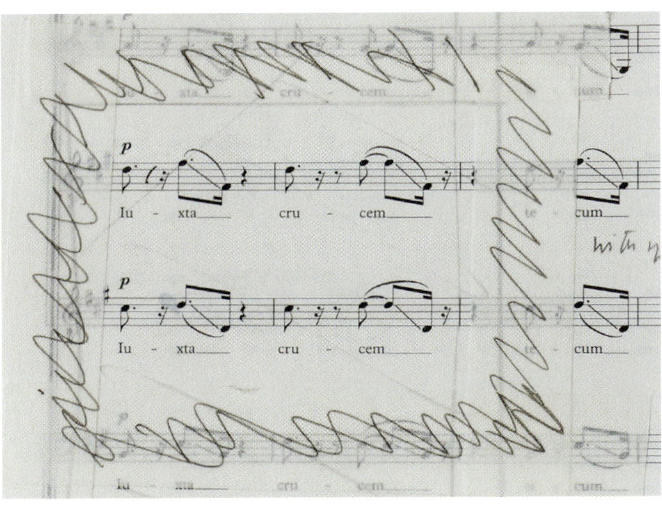

28. *Stabat Mater*, 2019 / Gabriel Jackson *Stabat Mater*, manuscript detail.

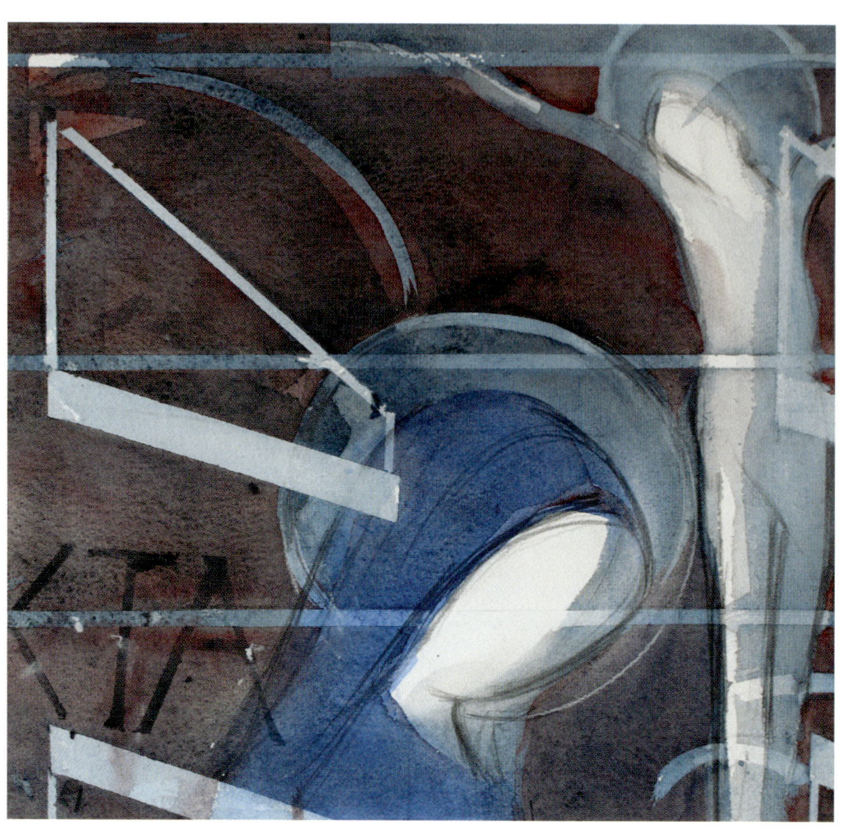

29. *Stabat Mater I*, 2018

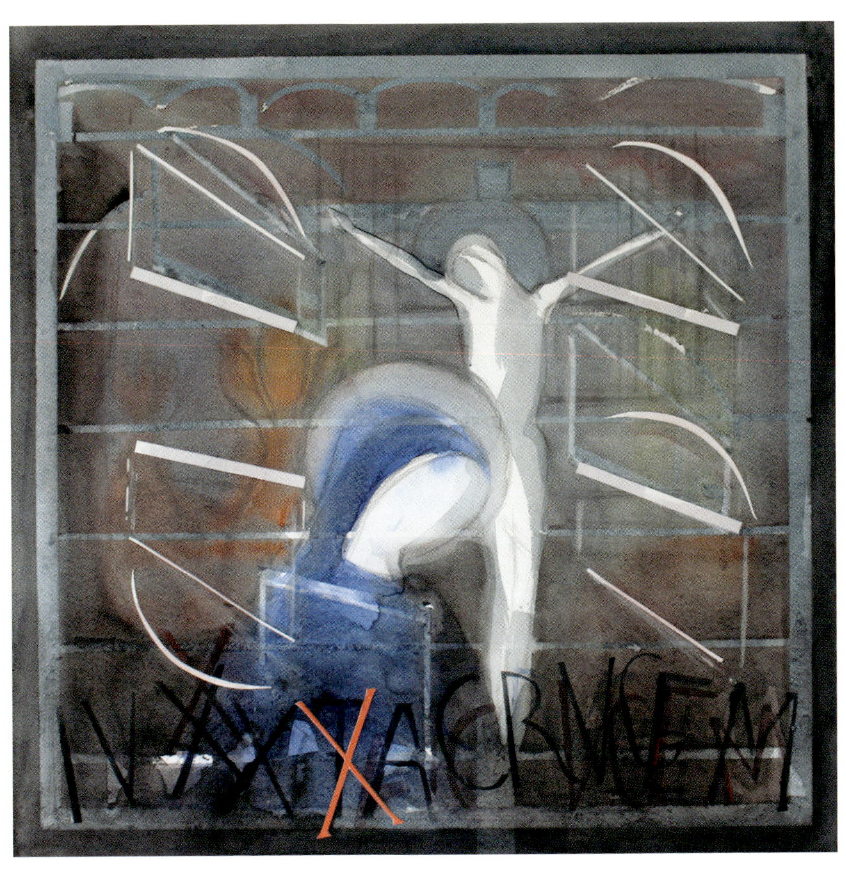

30. *Stabat Mater*, 2018

Magdalen College, Oxford

It was the association with Jonathan Arnold and his research into the subject of music and faith—specifically the contribution to the chapter on 'Eye Music' and my own religious beliefs, in his *Music and Faith: Conversations in a Post-Secular Age*—that led to an opportunity for a period of study at The Old Library, Magdalen College, and its collection of early manuscript fragments.

Studying these examples of various modes of musical notation, as well as attending services in the nearby college chapel, gradually led to an appreciation of participation in a religious service where the music is integral with the place, the liturgy and the ritual. Periods outside of worship were spent sitting in the choir, drawing and photographing the steep rows of choir stalls, with elaborate carved finials flanking a high altar set on wide steps and the massive stone reredos with ranks of vertical niches.

The underlying structural geometry of this intense interior—the diagonal, horizontal and vertical aspects—lent itself to the graphic characteristics of plainchant notation as expressed in *The Lamentations of Jeremiah* by Thomas Tallis, which was performed for the Good Friday liturgy in 2018. The music was, in some way, both contained within and absorbed by the presence of the chapel. In exaggerating the shapes of the notation, the persistence of slow and solemn tones is evoked, punctuated with high-pitched voices echoing throughout the spaces.

Another feature of the chapel choir are the Victorian stained glass windows, amongst which is a depiction of the Virgin and Child. The sideways tilt of the Virgin's head toward Jesus is strongly reminiscent of early Byzantine Art and Russian icons, and in several compositions this timeless subject—the detail of the faces simplified by the strong light—is integrated with a rhythmic palimpsest of free and expressive neumes.

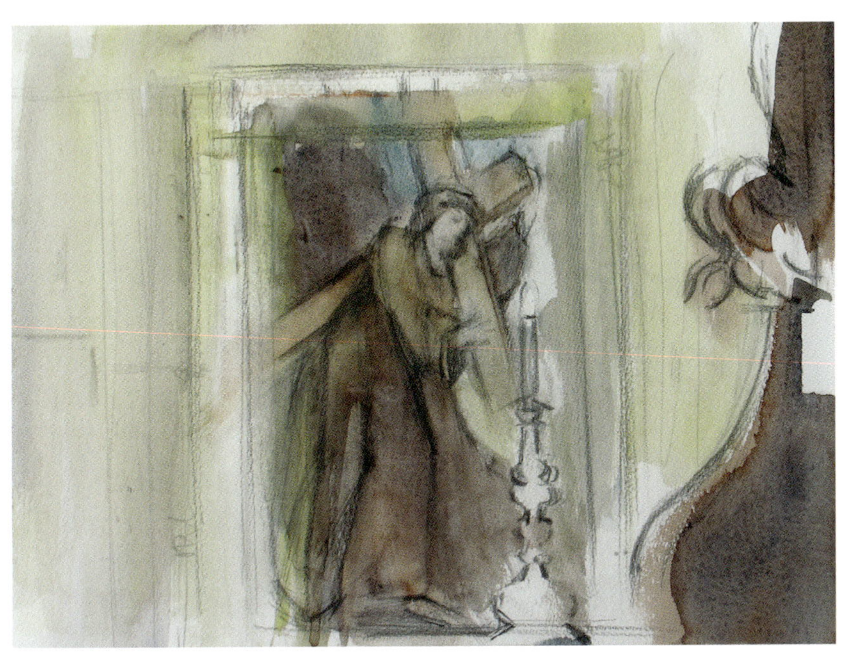

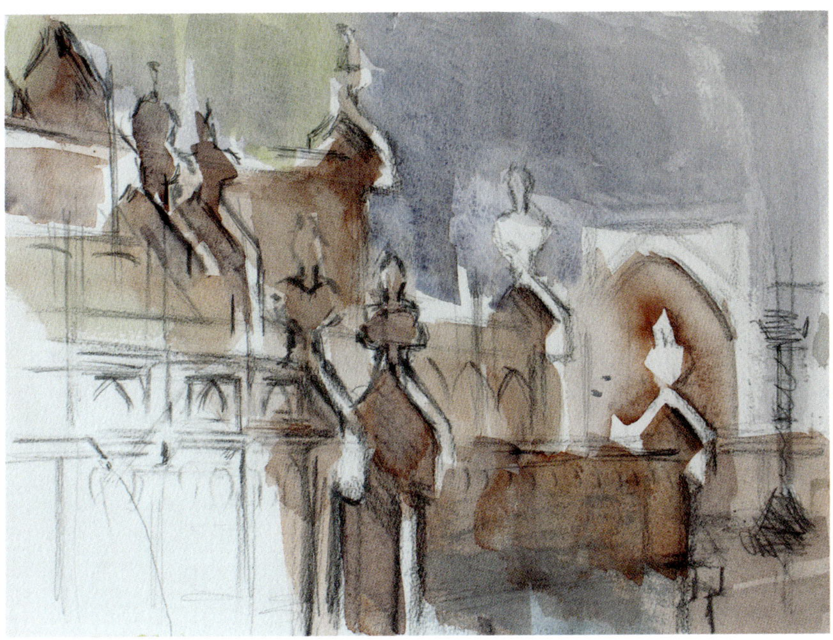

31. *Altarpiece*, 2017 | 32. *Choir stalls*, 2017

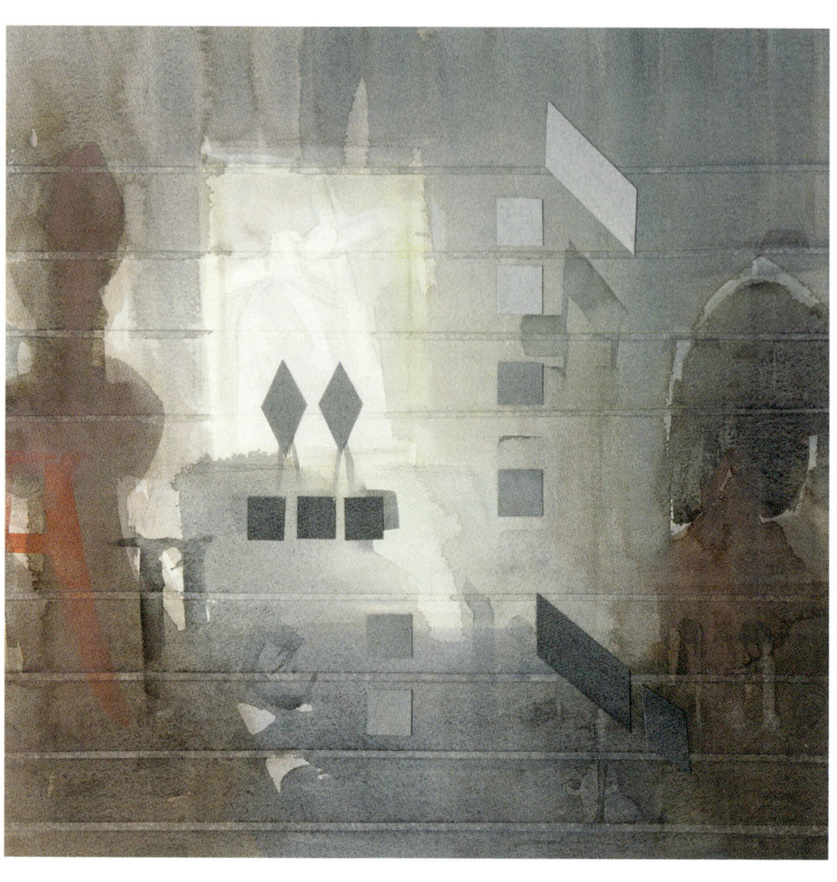

33. *Plainchant: Choral Evensong*, 2017

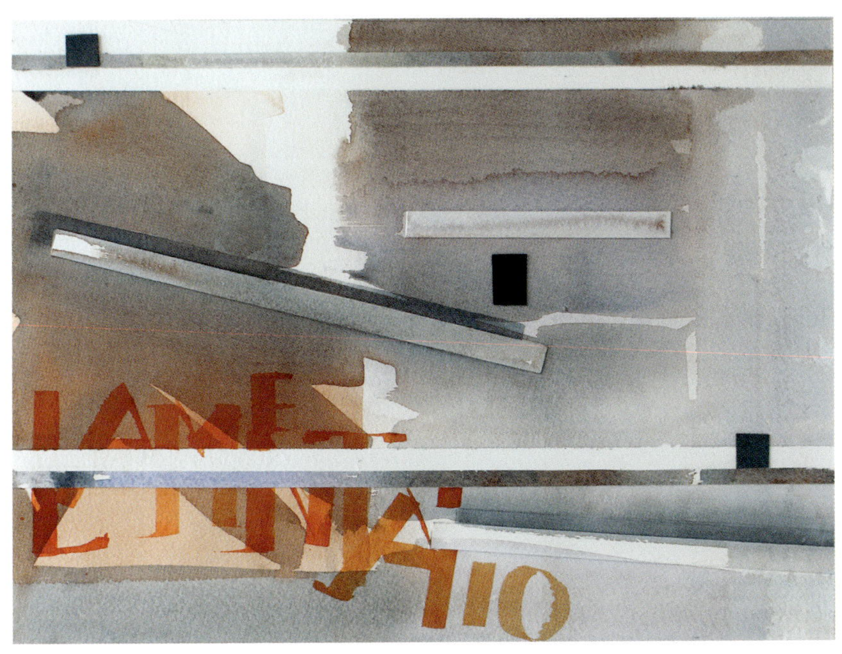

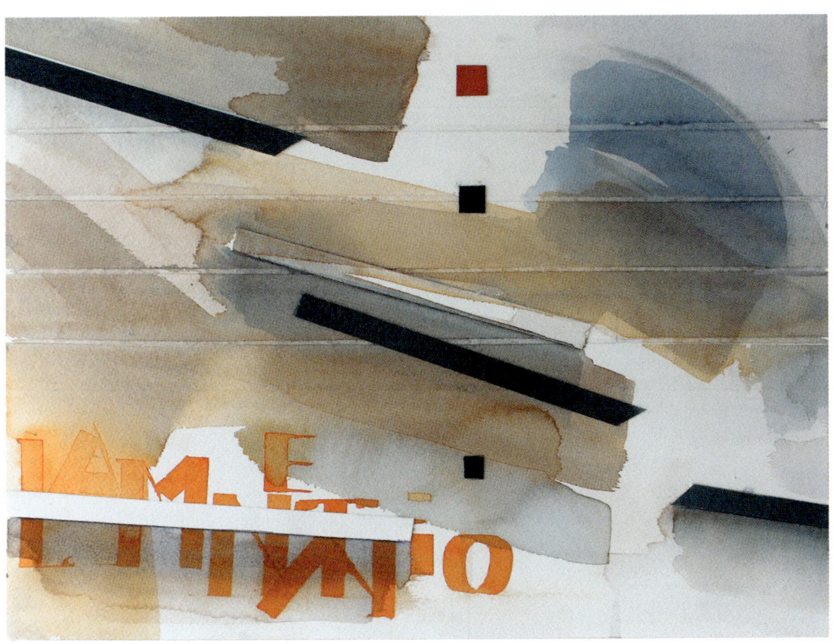

34. *Lamentations I*, 2019 / 35. *Lamentations II*, 2019

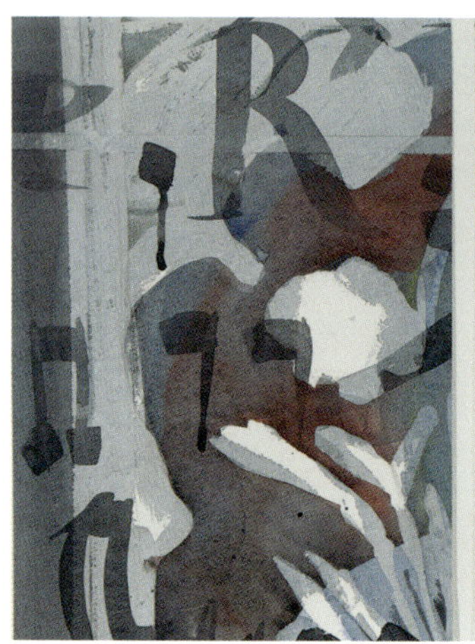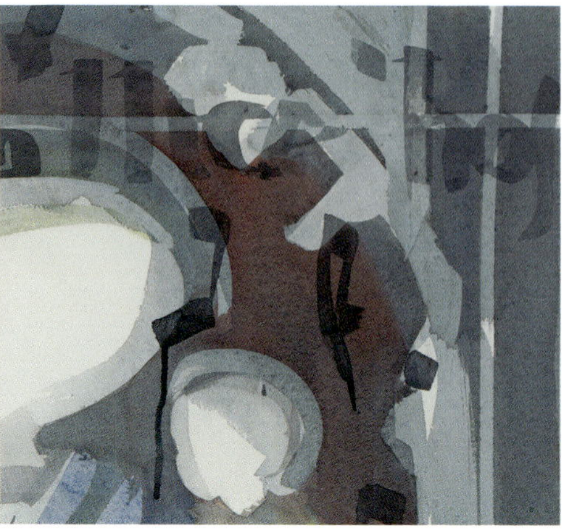

36. *Neumes: Virgin & Child, Study III*, 2017 / Manuscript with neumes

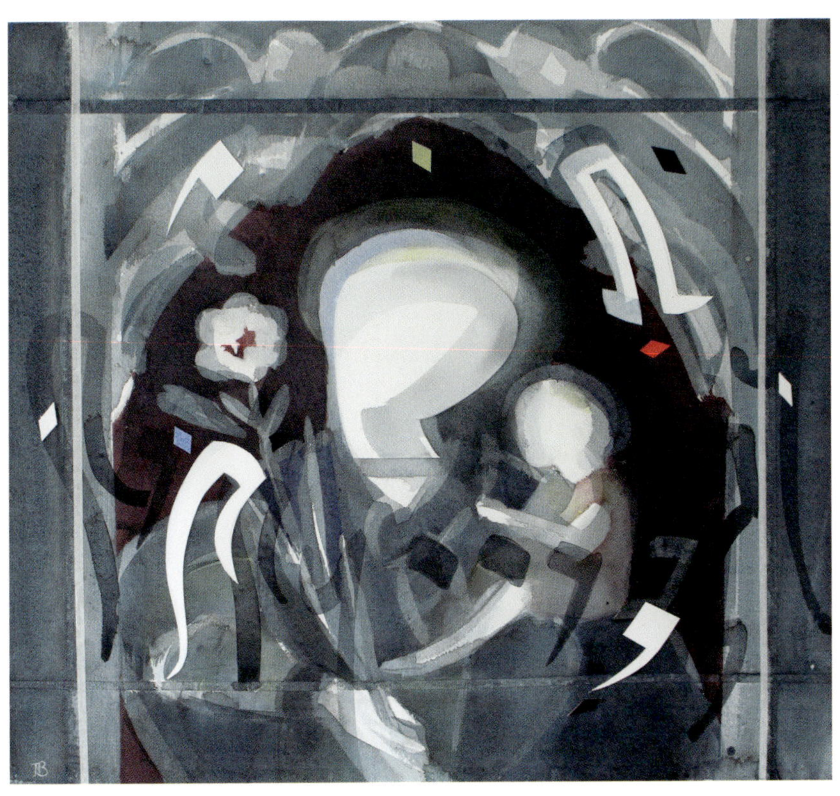

37. Neumes: Virgin & Child II, 2018

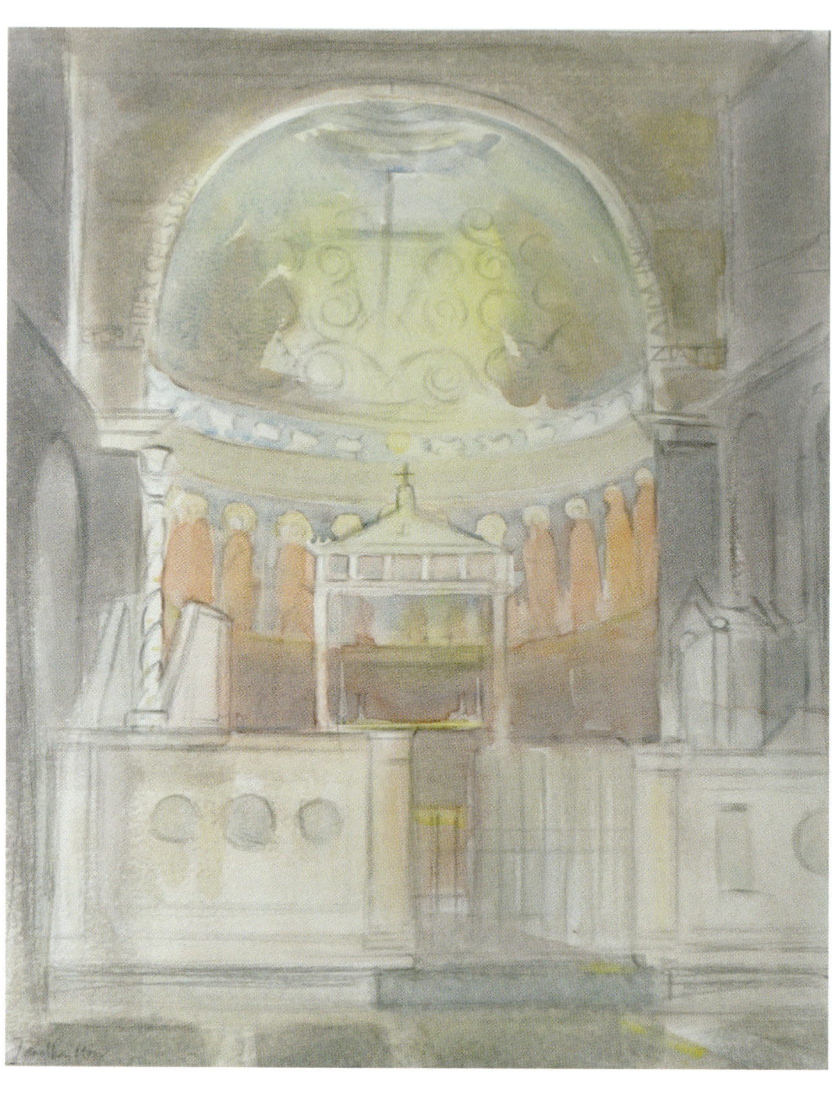

38. *Interior: Basilica di San Clemente, Rome*, 2009

Basilica of Saint Clemente, Rome

In 1989 I made a trip to Ravenna, Italy, to look at the fifth and sixth century Christian mosaics in the city's churches and convents. This was followed up with a visit to Rome in 1996 to seek out further examples of early Christian mosaics, mostly to be found fragmented and marginalised in obscure corners. I also went to the Basilica of San Clemente to look at the twelfth century apsidal mosaic which is thought in some ways to partly replicate a fourth or fifth century work which existed in the early church below. The twelfth century work was constructed in the context of Gregorian reform; a return to early Christian ideals.

In 2009 I returned to San Clemente as a guest of the Prior, Father Terence Crotty, with permission to draw, paint and photograph in the church. Attending services, observing and participating in the life of the Order of Dominicans and having access to the church from early morning to late evening, made for immersion in this exquisite enclave wedged between the Via Labicana and Via Di San Giovanni, a few hundred yards east of the Coliseum. The priory and church form two sides of a walled enclosure containing a small garden with

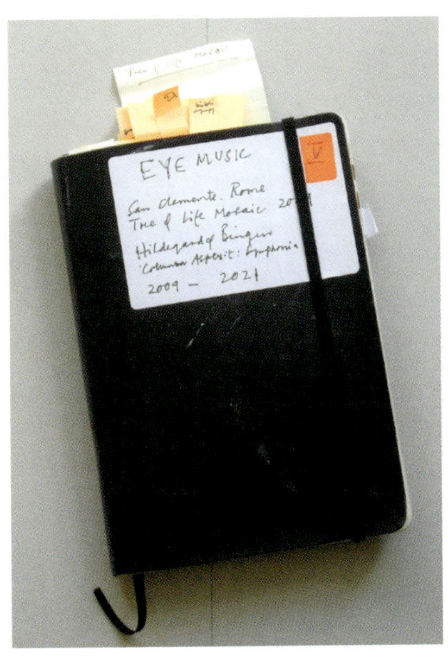

'Eye Music' notebook V, 2009–21

wild flowers, cedar and citrus trees, paved with seemingly random pieces of ancient marble, stone and brick.

Reading Fiona Maddock's biography *Hildegard of Bingen: The Woman of Her Age*, renewed interest in the life, art and music of the twelfth century German polymath. Although Hildegard never visited Italy she was well-versed and indeed influential in the activities of the wider church. Her own art and practice of Christianity indicates that she would have been in accord with the contemporary spirit of San Clemente.

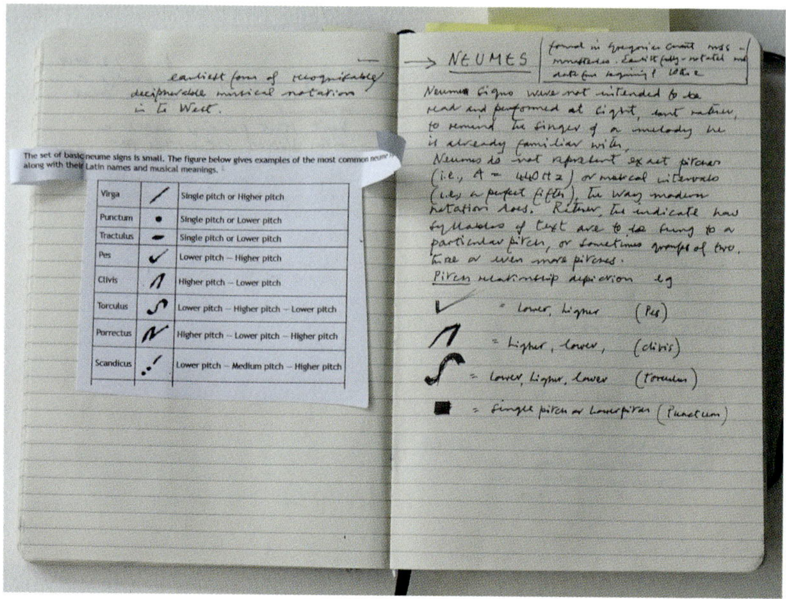

Set of basic neume symbols, 'Eye Music' notebook V, 2009–21

In 2019 I returned to the Basilica with the intention of re-establishing a concrete connection with its interior spaces and to focus on the particular area studied ten years earlier, looking east towards the schola cantorium, altar and mosaic in the apse. On this occasion it wasn't possible to make any further visual notes and being holiday time only an occasional abbreviated mass—without music—was held in a side chapel. These unforeseen limitations led to a few days of freedom, to sit and watch and wander unencumbered by the paraphernalia of art materials and camera. This enabled me to devote myself to understanding more about the life and art of the Mythraic temple and early Christian church in the excavations below, and spend time sitting in the elegant medieval forecourt which was once part of the main entrance; gaining a stronger sense of the whole history and life of the basilica since its earliest beginnings.

Choosing the manuscript page (opposite) of Hildegard of Bingen's hymn 'Columba Aspexit' from *Symphonia armonie celestium revelationum* (Symphony of the Celestial Harmonies), was determined not only by its interesting use of neumes and staves in the notation but because the text included 'Columba'—Dove, 'In Pectore'—Apostles, and 'Gemma'—Jewel/Bethlehem. These three words reminded me of some important images in the mosaic and fresco at San Clemente— doves surrounding Jesus on the Cross, depictions of Jerusalem and Bethlehem, and the fresco of the Twelve Apostles.

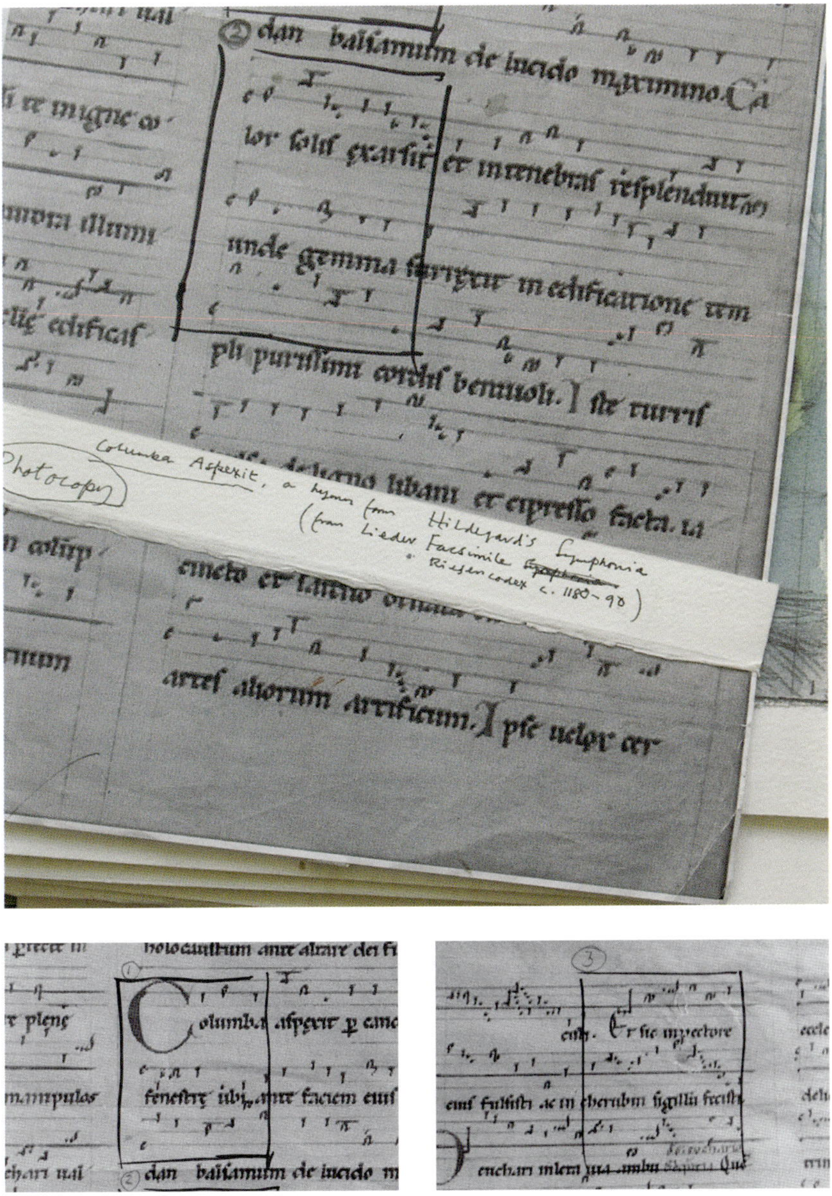

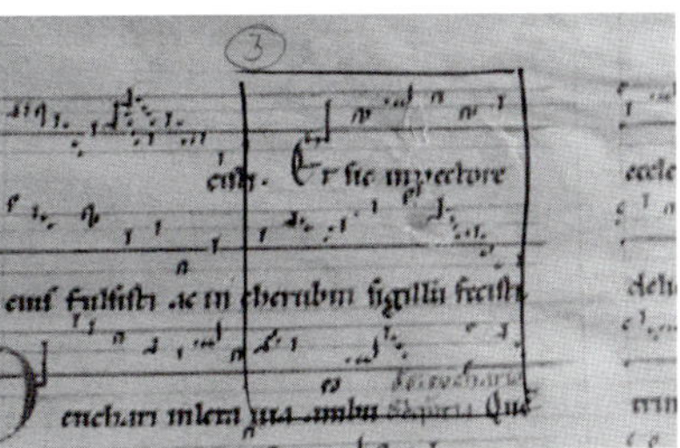

Workings (copy of Lieder Facsimile Riesen codex c.1180–90), 2019

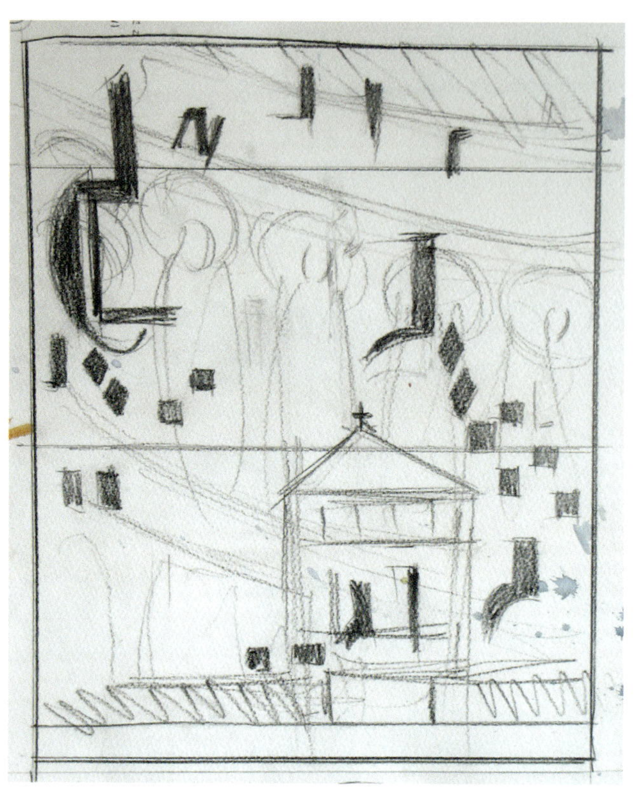

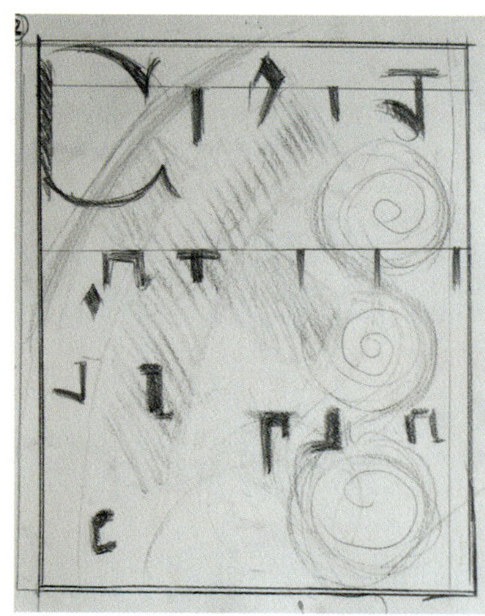

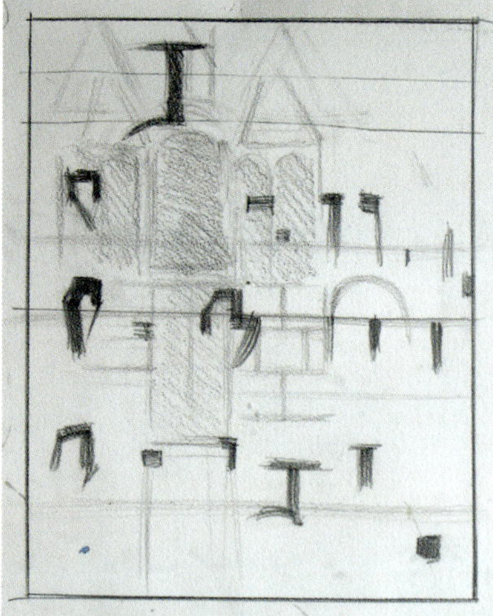

39–41. *The Apostles, The Tree of Life, Bethlehem, preliminary studies*, 2018

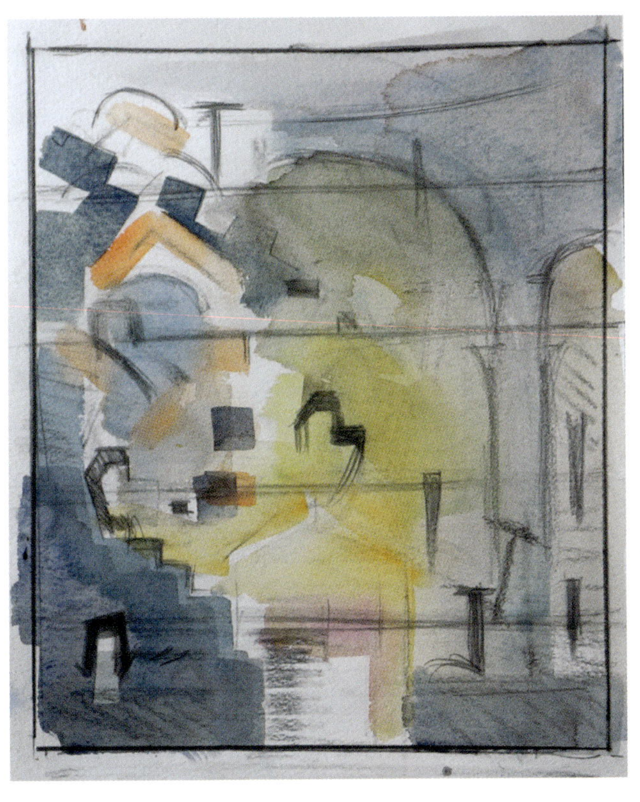

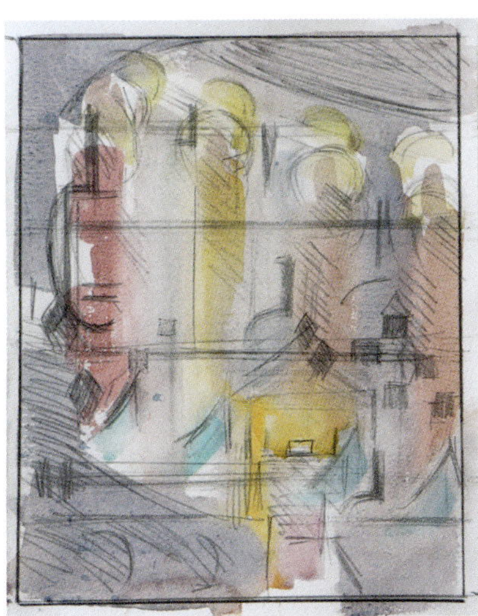

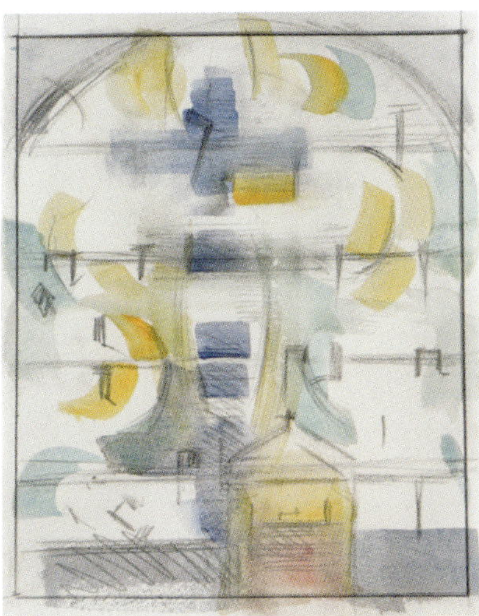

42–44. Bethlehem, *The Apostles*, *The Tree of Life*, preliminary studies, 2019

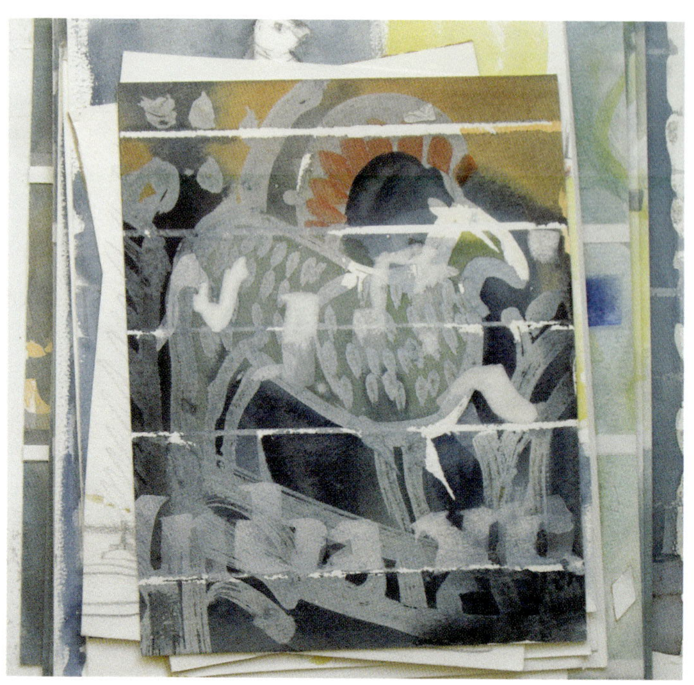

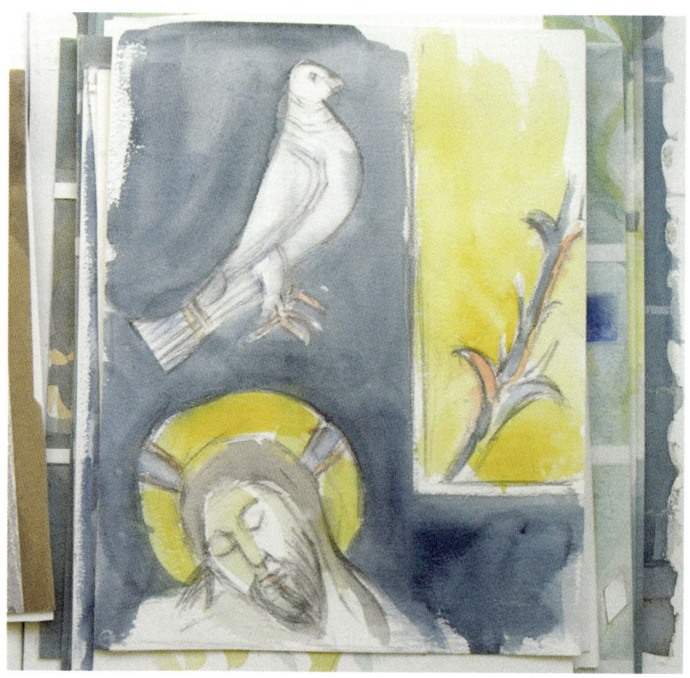

45–48. *The Tree of Life, San Clemente: apsidal mosaic, studies,* 2020

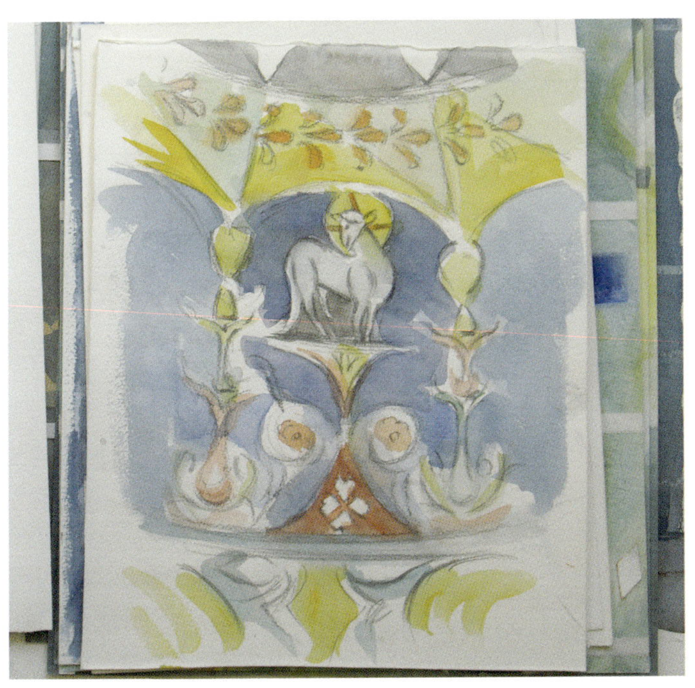

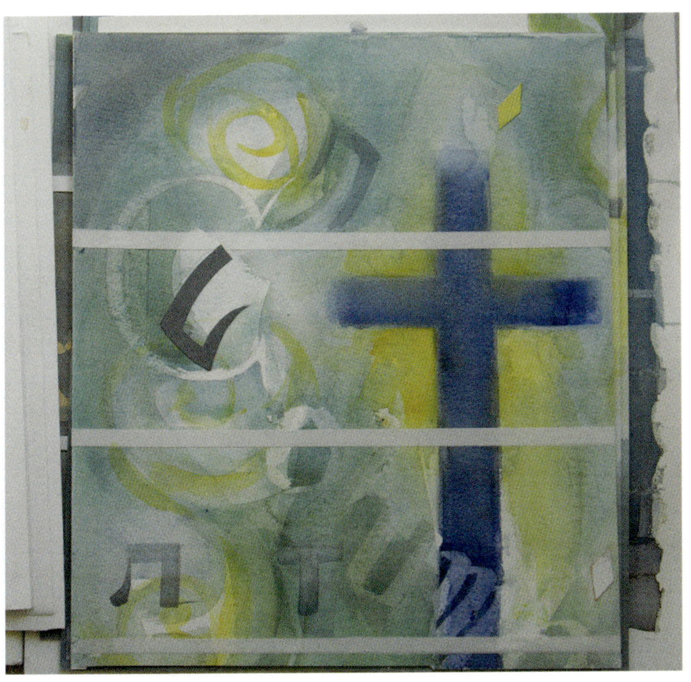

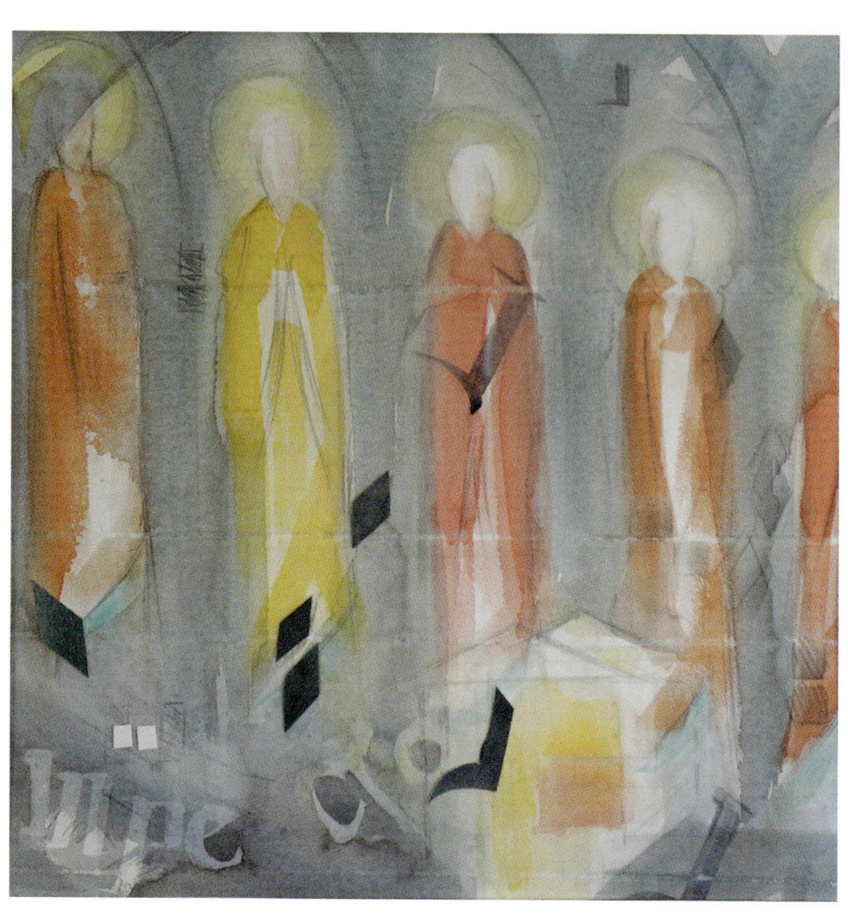

49. *The Apostles*, 2020

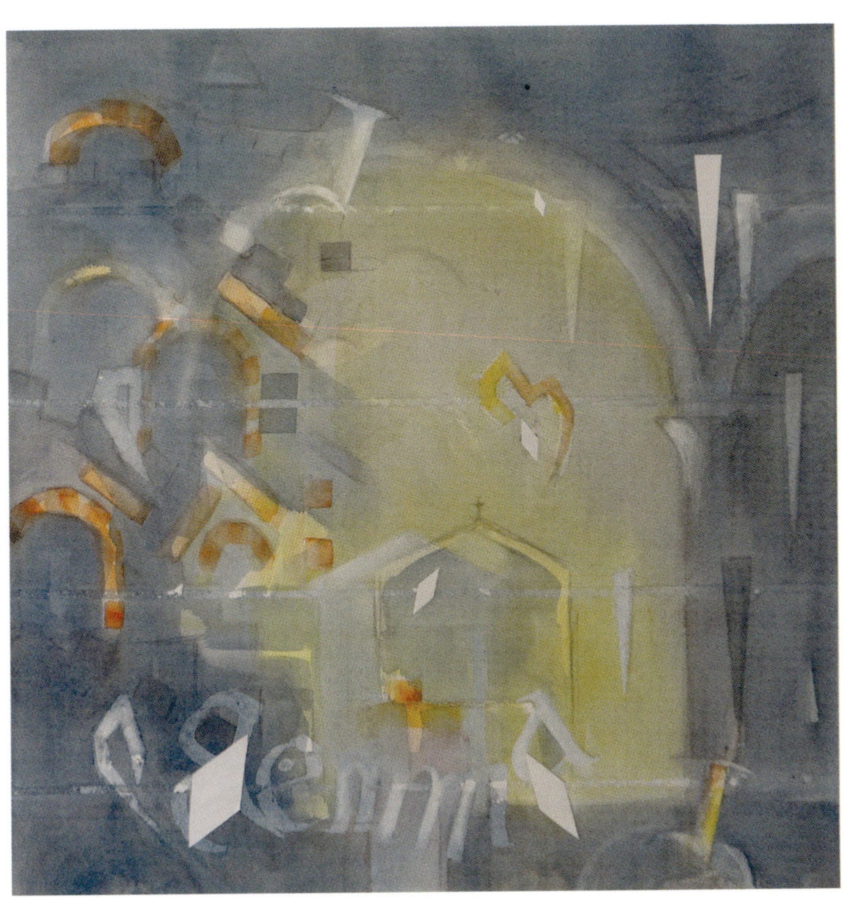

50. *Bethlehem*, 2020

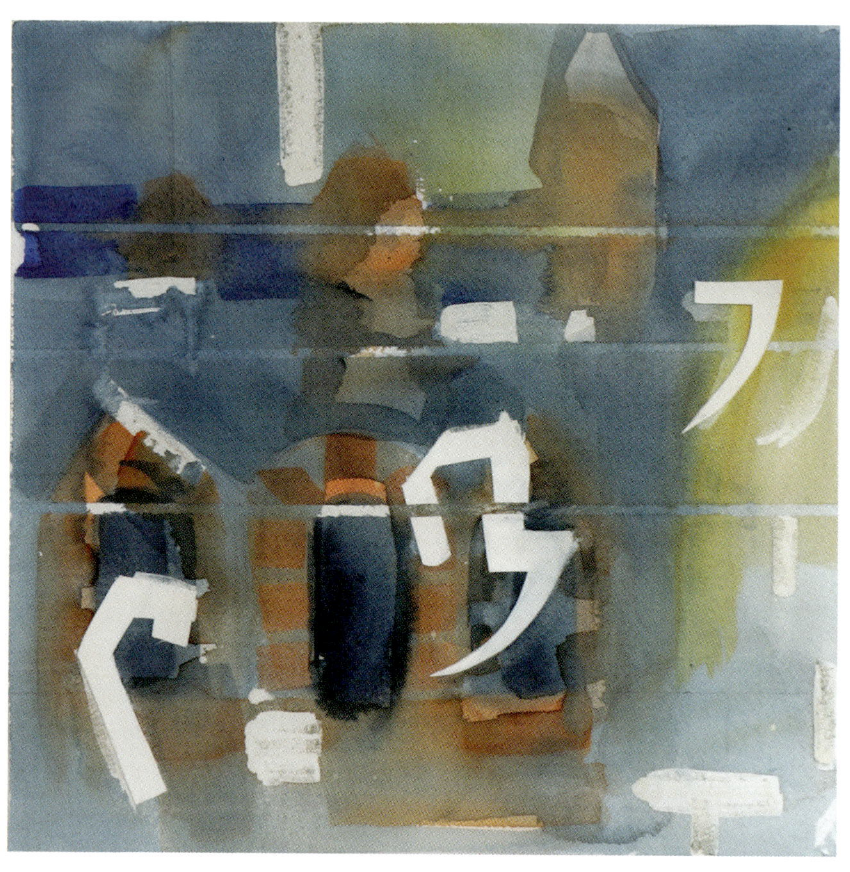

51. *Bethlehem*, 2021

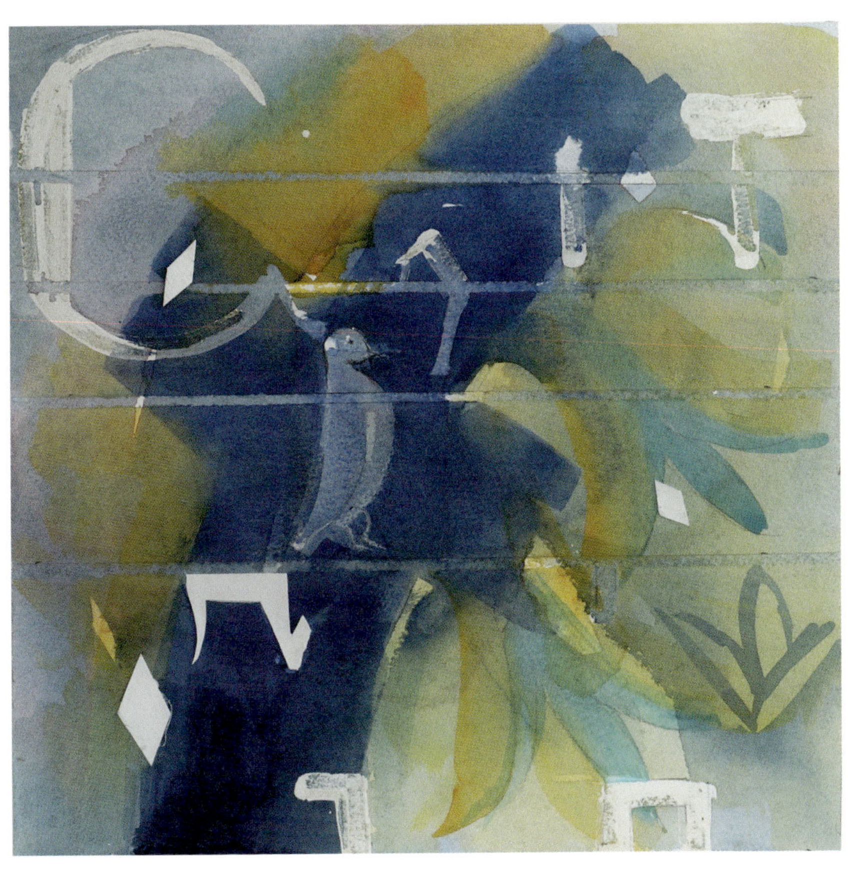

52. *The Tree of Life*, 2021

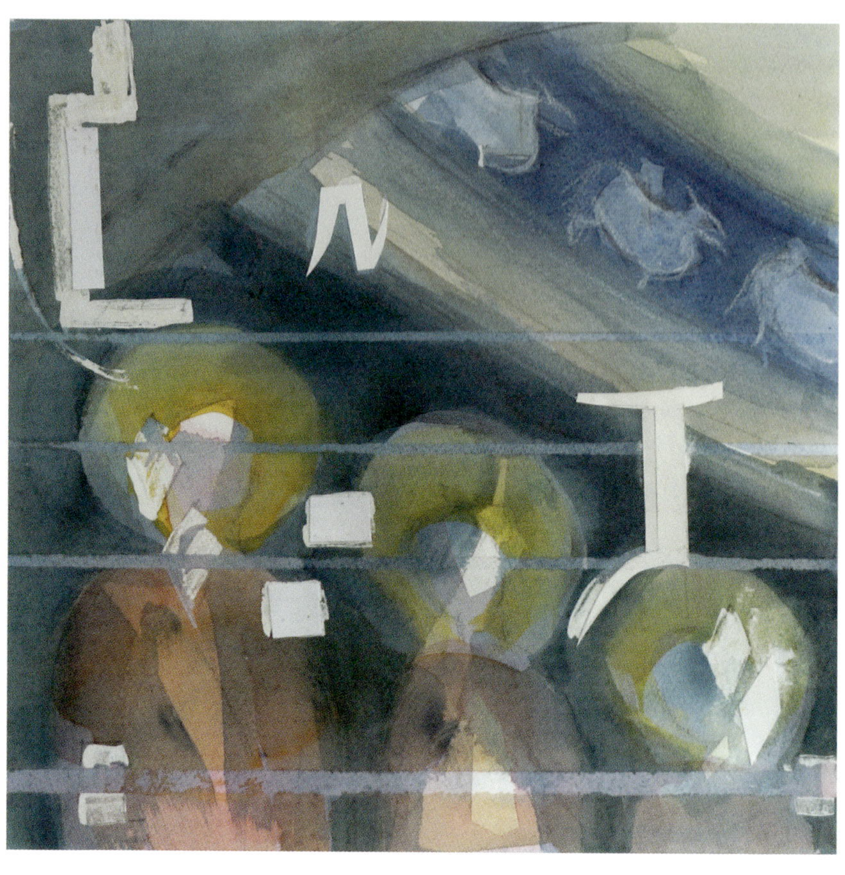

53. *The Apostles*, 2021

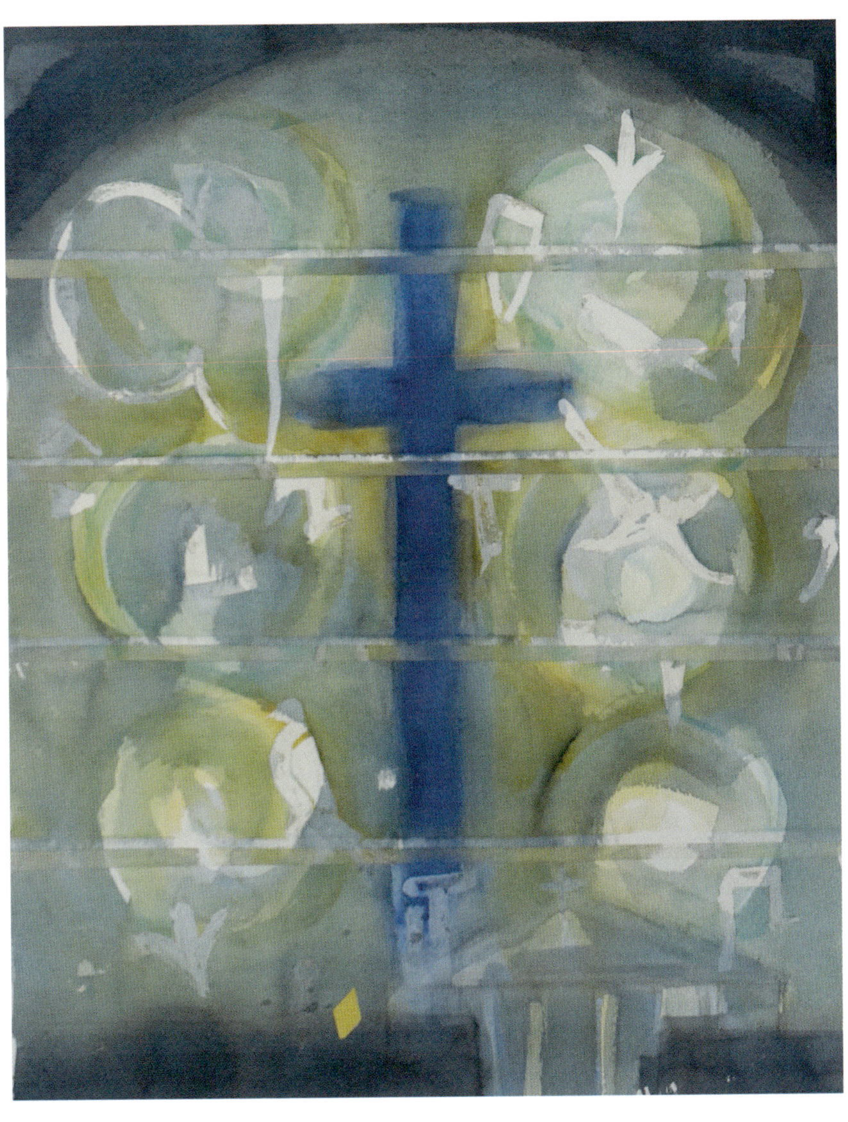

54. *The Tree of Life*, 2021

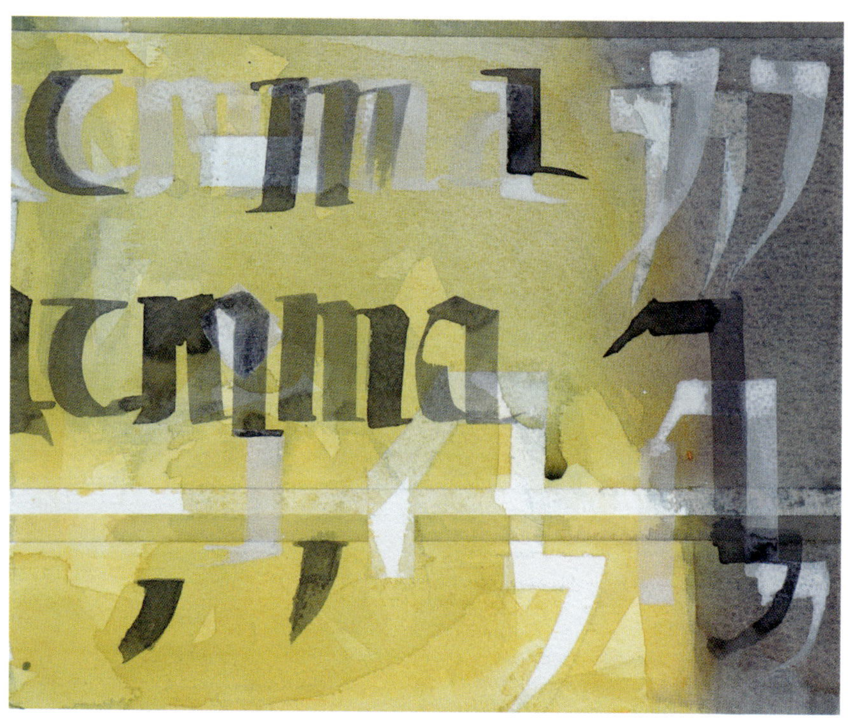

It is as if the flow of the music, as it travels along the forms of its notation on the page, has been held strangely suspended in both space and time, becoming almost tangible—Richard Morphet

55. From *The Book of Neumes*, 2021

Works

Preamble

1. *Generating Station, Diagram I*,
collage, 28 x 38, 1960
2. *Generating Station in
Landscape*, oil & acrylic on
board, 38 x 46, 1960
3. *Generating Station, January*,
collage, 60 x 60, 1961
4. *Generating Station, Spring*,
collage, 60 x 60, 1961
5. *Generating Station with
Concrete Posts*, oil on board,
56 x 60, 1961
6. *Generating Station, Diagram II*,
collage, 26 x 30, 1961
7. *View of Generating Station*,
monoprint, 18 x 20, 1961

Still Life

8. *Early Study I*, watercolour
& collage, 45 x 45, 2004
9. *Early Study II*, watercolour
& collage, 45 x 45, 2004
10. *Early Music I*, paperpulp
collage, 74 x 80, 2005
11. *Early Music II*, paperpulp
collage, 74 x 80, 2005

Construction

12. *Jam Jars in a Window*,
watercolour & collage,
42 x 42, 2005
13. *Jam Jars in a Window,
Pink & Turquoise*, watercolour
& collage, 82 x 77, 2006–11
14. *Jam Jars in a Window,
Green & Terracotta*, watercolour
& collage, 86 x 82, 2006–14

15. *Jam Jars in a Window,
Green & Terracotta*, watercolour
& collage, 58 x 58, 2011
16. *Study I, Blue & Green*,
watercolour & collage,
28 x 28, 2011
17. *Study V, Blue & Green*,
watercolour & collage,
30 x 39, 2014
18. *Study VII, Blue & Green*,
watercolour & collage,
30 x 41, 2014

Keble College Library, Oxford

19. *Drawn Scores*, pencil,
108 x 38, 2013
20. *Early Music*, pencil,
15 x 60, 2013
21. *Untitled*, paperpulp,
14 x 22, 2013
22. *Red Missale I, 1514*,
paperpulp, 108 x 38, 2013

Blackfriars Priory, Oxford

23. *Tenebrae II*, watercolour
& collage, 28 x 28, 2016
24. *Tenebrae III*, watercolour
& collage, 34 x 48, 2016
25. *Tenebrae IV*, watercolour
& collage, 38 x 44, 2016
26. *Tenebrae*, watercolour
& collage, 65 x 65, 2017
27. *Tenebrae V*, watercolour
& collage, 40 x 44, 2018

Merton College Chapel, Oxford

28. *Stabat Mater*, watercolour
& collage, 58 x 62, 2018

29. *Stabat Mater I*, watercolour
& collage, 35 x 36, 2018
30. *Stabat Mater*, watercolour
& collage, 76 x 76, 2018

Magdalen College, Oxford

31. *Altarpiece*, watercolour
& pencil, 30 x 40, 2017
32. *Choir stalls*, watercolour
& pencil, 30 x 40, 2017
33. *Plain Chant: Choral
Evensong*, watercolour
& collage, 45 x 45, 2017
34. *Lamentations I*, watercolour
& collage, 33 x 45, 2019
35. *Lamentations II*, watercolour
& collage, 33 x 45, 2019
36. *Neumes: Virgin & Child III*,
watercolour & collage,
38 x 66, 2017
37. *Neumes: Virgin & Child III*,
watercolour & collage,
57 x 62, 2018

Basilica of Saint Clemente,
Rome

38. *Interior: Basilica di San
Clemente, Rome*, watercolour,
58 x 45, 2009
39–41. *The Apostles, The Tree
of Life, Bethlehem, preliminary
studies*, pencil, each 40 x 30,
2018
42–44. *Bethlehem, The Apostles,
The Tree of Life, preliminary
studies*, pencil & watercolour,
each 40 x 30, 2019
45–48. *The Tree of Life, San
Clemente: apsidal mosaic,
studies*, pencil & watercolour,
each 31 x 40, 2020

49. *The Apostles*, watercolour
& collage, 75 x 60, 2020
50. *Bethlehem*, watercolour
& collage, 68 x 66, 2020
51. *Bethlehem*, watercolour
& collage, 38 x 38, 2021
52. *The Tree of Life*, watercolour
& collage, 38 x 38, 2021
53. *The Apostles*, watercolour
& collage, 38 x 38, 2021
54. *The Tree of Life*, watercolour
& collage, 71 x 55, 2020
55. From *The Book of Neumes*,
watercolour, 27 x 32, 2021

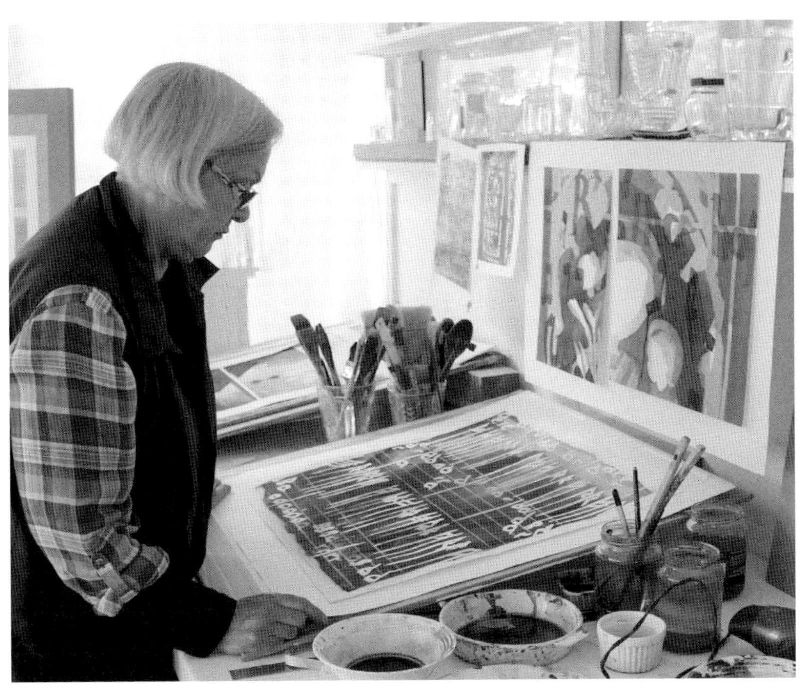

Studio, Abingdon, 2017

Readings

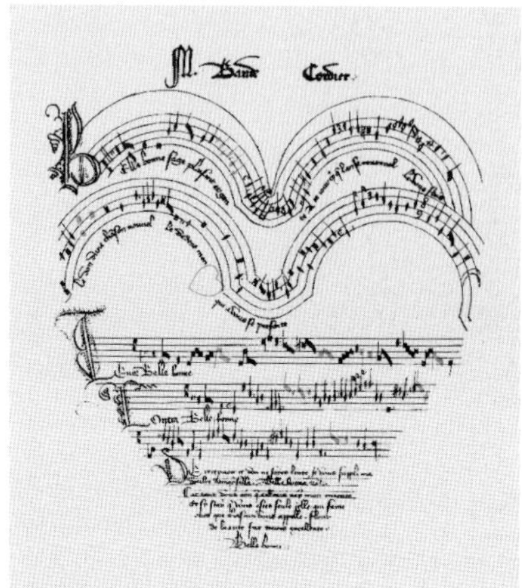 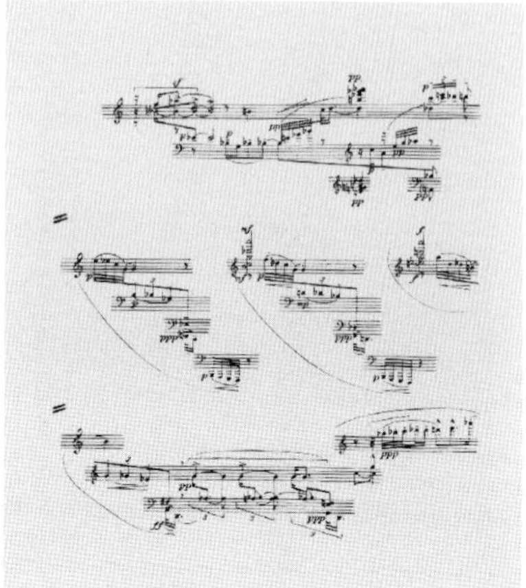

The score (above left) is a love song where the staves have been bent
to represent a heart. It is an early example of *Augenmusik* or Eye
Music, by the Italian Renaissance composer Baude Cordier in 1400.
The shape is emblematic of the meaning and mood of part of the
song. Another expressive visual device used in this early period of
developments in musical notation was to depict the themes of 'death'
and 'night' with black note-heads, and those about 'light' and 'life'
with white notes.

In 1915 the Russian composer Arthur Lourié in his score for solo
piano entitled *Formes en l'Air* (above right), cut away sections of the
staves leaving blank gaps to represent the all-important passages of
silence, thus making the overall appearance of the music on the page
lighter and more airy. In this way the manuscript becomes visually
expressive of the subject and open to a freer, individualistic interpretation by the performer.

I wonder if the American poet, Mary Ellen Solt, was familiar with
Lourié's score when she wrote the two-part poem, *Dogwood: Three
movements*, 1965 (opposite, left). The International Concrete Poetry
Movement, which was concerned with the visual and graphical potential of poetry, was first established in Brazil in the nineteen-fifties at
the same time as the American composer John Cage was eschewing
the conventions of notation and presenting a musical score pictorially.
In a similar way, the work of the concrete poets challenged the traditional poetic elements of regular measures and rhythms.

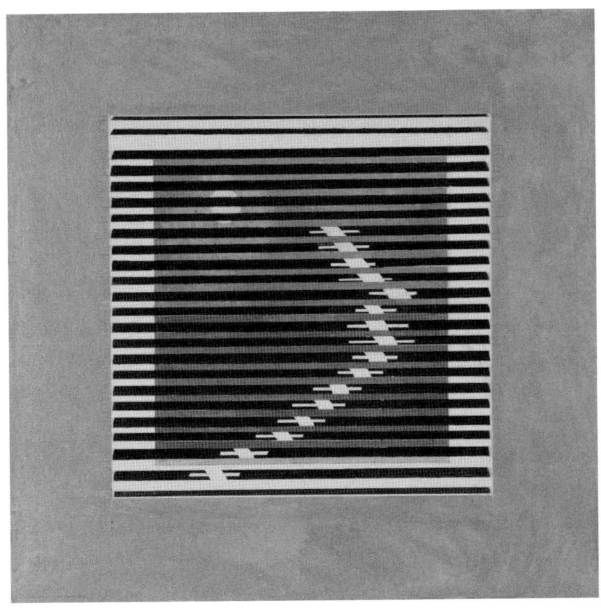

In 1986 I came across a catalogue for the Arts Council touring exhibition *Eye Music: The Graphic Art of New Musical Notation*. It contains a concise well-illustrated account of the history of this art form from twelfth-century China to the present. At some time in the following year I saw a reproduction of the poster/poem *Star/Steer* by Ian Hamilton Finlay (below right). It reminded me of a painting I had made in 1972 called *Moonlight on a Venetian Blind* (above). Both the Finlay screenprint and my painting of the reflection are night scenes in grey and faux-silver.

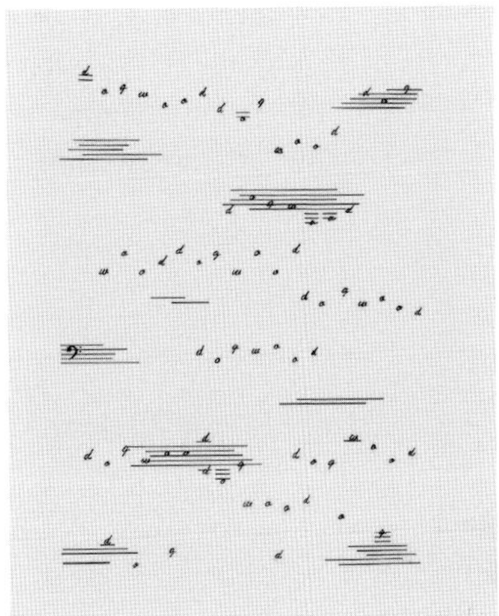

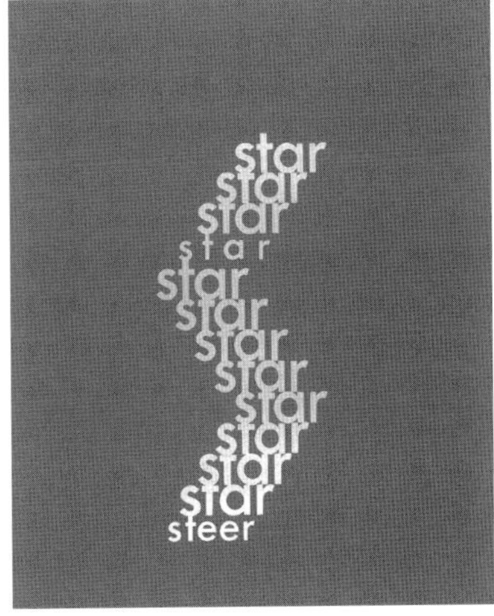

Bibliography

Mary Ellen Solt, ed., *Concrete Poetry: A World View* (Indiana University Press, 1968)

Gardner Read, *Music Notation: A Manual of Modern Practice* (Victor Gollancz, 1974)

Yves Abrioux, *Ian Hamilton Finlay: A Visual Primer* (Reaktion Books, 1986)

Hugh Davies, Julie Lawson, Michael Regan, *Eye Music: The Graphic Art of New Musical Notation* (Arts Council, 1986)

Andrew Wilson-Dickson, *The story of Christian music, from Gregorian chant to Black gospel: an authoritative illustrated guide to all the major traditions of music for worship* (Lion Publishing, 1992)

Hajo Duchting, *Paul Klee: Painting Music* (Prestel Verlag, 1997)

B. H. Friedman, ed., *Give my regards to Eighth Street: Collected Writings of Morton Feldman* (Exact Change, 2000)

David Nicholls, Jonathan Cross, eds., *The Cambridge Companion to John Cage* (Cambridge University Press, 2002)

Leo Black, *Franz Schubert: Music and Belief* (Boydell Press, 2003)

Theresa Sauer, *Notations 21* (Mark Batty, 2009)

Frances Guy, Simon Shaw-Miller, Michael Tucker, *Eye-Music: Kandinsky, Klee and All that Jazz* (Pallant House Press, 2007)

Willi Apel, *The Notation of Polyphonic Music, 900–1600* (Oxford City Press, 2010)

Peter Vergo, *The Music of Painting: Music, Modernism and the Visual Arts from the Romantics to John Cage* (Phaidon, 2011)

Jonathan Arnold, *Sacred Music in Secular Society* (Routledge, 2014)

Christopher de Hamel, *Meetings with Remarkable Manuscripts* (Allen Lane, 2016)

David Nicholas Buck, *A Musicality for Landscape* (Routledge, 2017)

Jonathan Arnold, *Music and Faith: Conversations in a Post-Secular Age* (Boydell Press, 2019)

Fiona Maddocks, *Hildegard of Bingen: The Woman of Her Age* (Headline Books, 2019)

Joe Scarffe, 'Conceptualising Musical Graphic Performance: An Investigative Journey of Self-Reflective Artistic Practice and Auto-ethnography', PhD Thesis (Royal Birmingham Conservatoire, 2019)

Giovanni Varelli, ed., *Disiecta Membra Musicae: Studies in Musical Fragmentology* (Walter de Gruyter, 2020)

Nancy Perloff, ed., *Concrete Poetry: A 21st-Century Anthology* (Reaktion Books, 2022)

Joe Scarffe
An Introduction to 'Eye Music'

In the last sixty years, everything from military maps to telephone
doodles have been used to score music. Everyone from the American
composer John Cage to The Beatles have sought new methods of
communicating music for which traditional music notation was not
adequate. In 1969, John Cage published a book called *Notations* that
contained hundreds of examples of these scores, demonstrating the
extent of their abundance and variety. In 2009, the New York-based
composer and researcher, Theresa Sauer, published *Notations 21*—
comprising over one hundred composers' works written since 1969
—marking the fortieth anniversary of Cage's book.

With such an overwhelming variety of scores and notation systems
available, how do performers and audiences even begin to make sense
of it all? This question has been the focus of my research for the last
five years, indeed, it was at a pre-concert talk on this subject that I
first met Janet Boulton. These issues will be explored, in relation to the
'Eye Music' series, later in this introduction, but it is first necessary to
explain how these scores are categorised and defined, and the issues
they present for both composers and performers.

Ever since music was first written down, the relationship between
its visual appearance and its ability to communicate music has been
constantly evolving, as composers have sought to express increasingly
complex musical ideas and new relationships between scores and
performers. From Babylonian stone tablets to Ancient Egyptian Colour
Music, there was an abundance of unique approaches to notating
music across the ancient world. Indeed, it is important to realise that
it was only in 1000 AD that a monk called Guido of Arezzo created
the staff notation that became the global standardised system we use
today.

In the fifteenth century, composers began to embellish and add
visual interest to their scores to enhance the expressive impact of the
music. Baude Cordier presented the stave lines in his love song collection, *Belle, Bonne, Sage*, in the shape of a heart, and others painted
biblical or mythological scenes as part of their scores. This practice is
known as Augenmusik or Eye Music and can still be seen today in the
work of George Crumb, Claudia Molitor and Brent Michael-Davids.

In the twentieth century, there has been an explosion of new
approaches to notating music, as composers began to use visual art
not to just embellish the score, but become the notation itself. These

new approaches can be roughly divided into Graphic Music Notation, which is either fixed or indeterminate, and Musical Graphics that blur the boundary between notation and visual art and require the performer to use them as a stimulus from which to improvise. The term 'Musical Graphics' was coined in 1959 by the Polish composer Roman Haubenstock-Ramati, for the first-ever exhibition of graphic scores, in Donaueschingen, Germany.

These new score categories were first discussed in detail in Erhard Karkoschka's seminal book, *Notation in New Music*. Here, Karkoschka defines graphic notation as having the usual coordinates of time and space, comprising more symbols than drawing and proceeding from a linear representation. Musical graphics, on the other hand, are defined by lacking these fundamental elements. Therefore, under Karkoschka's definition, the works presented in this book are all musical graphics. As Boulton is primarily an artist and the 'Eye Music' series has not included performance notes, these works can also be appropriately described as autonomous. By this, I mean that the works are intended to be enjoyed both purely as visual art and as a stimulus to improvise from. This autonomy is a fundamental aspect of many musical graphics because, in the words of Julia Schroder, "musical graphics are composed not with the intent of producing concrete music; they may, however, be translated into music". Karkoschka is critical of musical graphics, for this reason, and describes them as utopian, and he is not alone in this view. John Evarts even goes as far as saying that one day we might be seeing ensembles playing Picasso's *Guernica*.

However, Karkoschka does later admit that works which spread the boundary between visual art, literature and music are fruitful and that "to regard such works with suspicion would betray one's sensitivity". Indeed, staff notation can be extremely beautiful, but Sylvia Smith suggests that the only reason we don't take much interest in its visual qualities is because "it is too clearly recognisable as notation—it is too familiar to take an interest in".

The first musical graphic ever written was Earle Brown's *December 1952*, made up of thirty-one differently-sized black lines on a white background:

> My first thoughts about making music works in what I call a condition of mobility and what is now called open form, were influenced by the mobiles of the American sculptor Alexander Calder. At approximately the same time, around 1948, the paintings and working methods of Jackson Pollock began to be widely publicised in America. A correlation that I made—rightly

or wrongly—between these two artists and their technical and aesthetic points of view has been my rather obsessive primary motivation as an artist and composer since that time.

December 1952 is the first work that allowed the performers to start and end at any position and move wherever they like within the score. This mobility and open form character reflect Brown's jazz background, as well as his visual art and sculptural influences.

There is a clear connection between the open form character and mobility of *December 1952* and the 'Eye Music' series. The only difference is that, rather than depicting a 3D mobile, Janet's work originates from a still life installed in a window, comprising five glass shelves and rows of jam jars. She has said to me that she became increasingly aware of the co-relation of music and tone, so much so that sometimes it was as if sounds were playing back to her while she was painting. Through the process of creating the 'Eye Music' series, she began to understand the importance of the spatial aspect of music.

As Brown and Boulton have explored a similar concept from such different backgrounds and with such different skill sets, an important issue to raise is whether musical graphics are more effective at stimulating musical responses than non-musical graphics. The composer Roman Haubenstock-Ramati was questioned about this at the first-ever conference on graphic scores at the Darmstadt Music Conference, in 1964. His response was that there are many paintings by artists such as Wassily Kandinsky and Paul Klee that are overtly musical in appearance and even use musical terminology, but have never been performed. Musical graphics, on the other hand, are intended to be played by musicians and thus are often performed. For Ramati, this was an indication that it is both the fact that they have been created by musicians and their intention to be viewed as a stimulus for improvisation, that makes them explicitly musical and thus more effective at stimulating musicians than non-musical graphics.

Despite this, when looking through the collection of works in this book, it might seem that they are divorced entirely from not just music notation but music altogether. However, it is important to recognise that performing these works requires one to be responsible for generating the musical content as well as performing it and therefore no two performances of the work will be recognisably alike. For artists and composers, this concept of representing an existing text or painting in an original work is not new, and is known as *ekphrasis*. 'However, in her book, *Musical Ekphrasis*, Siglund Bruhn is hesitant to say that musical graphics are "integrations of music and picture", but, in the case of Boulton's work, it is hard to see them as anything else.

This is what makes her 'Eye Music' series of images such an interesting recent development in her work. Musicians are able to create their own visual and sonic integration of her still life, with its reference to plainchant, and explore the complex relationship at the heart of all of Janet Boulton's work, between the abstract and the concrete.

References

Siglund Bruhn, *Musical Ekphrasis* (Pendragon Press, 2000) / John Cage, *Notations* (Something Else Press, 1969) / John Evarts, 'The new musical notation: a graphic art?' *Leonardo* 1/4 (1968) / Roman Haubenstock-Ramati and Katherine Freeman, 'Notation—material and form', *Perspectives of New Music* 4/1 (1965) / Erhard Karkoschka, *Notation in New Music: A Critical Guide to Interpretation and Realisation* (Praeger, 1972) / Theresa Sauer, *Notations 21* (Mark Batty, 2009) / Julia Schröder, 'Graphic Notation and Musical Graphics: Between Music Notation and Visual Art', Daniels and Naumannm eds, *See This Sound, Audiovisuology Compendium* (Walter König, 2010) / Sylvia Smith, 'Visual music', *Perspectives of New Music*. 20/1 (1981)

Joe Scarffe

Janet Boulton's studio, Spring Road, Abingdon; October 2013

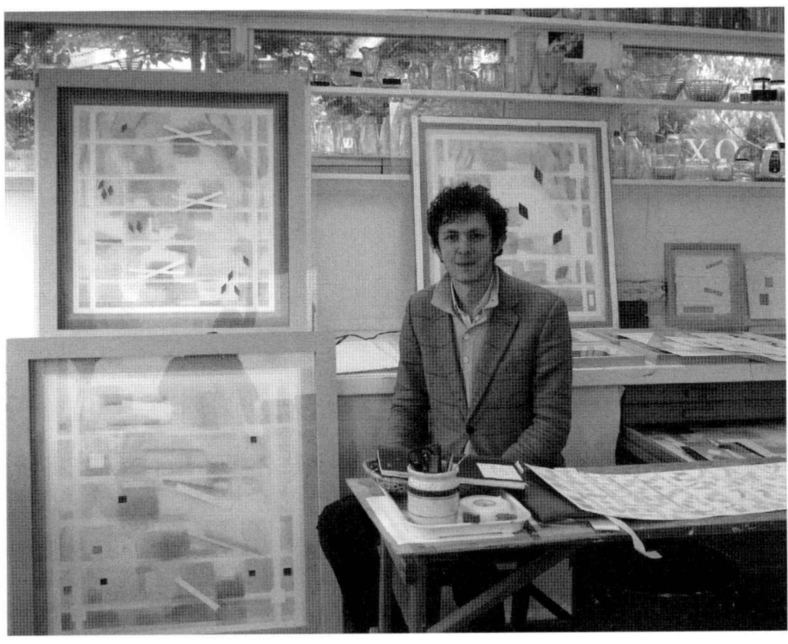

I first met Janet at a presentation I made on the history of graphic
scores at St John's Church in Oxford in 2013. Speaking briefly after the
event, it was clear to me that we shared many interests and perspectives regarding graphic scores. I then made a visit to her studio where
she showed me some of the 'Eye Music' series and I was immediately
captivated by them.

At the time I was in the early stages of my PhD research at the Royal
Birmingham Conservatoire, which was focussed on how performers
engage with musical graphics: an abstract type of graphic score which
typically contain little or no instructions for how to perform them.
I decided to use several of the 'Eye Music' series as one of the case
studies for my thesis both because they are all musical graphics and
I was intrigued by the references to plainchant and the jam jars in
Janet's studio. I also felt that Janet and I were on related investigative
enquiries in our creative work, with opposing trajectories. Whereas
Janet expressed to me that she felt as though she was learning about
sound, through the creation of the 'Eye Music' series, I felt that
performing musical graphics was teaching me how to interpret visual
artistic space, colour and texture.

The performance took place in Janet's studio and involved the composer and multi-instrumentalist, Samuel Rodgers. We performed *Jam Jars in a Window: Grey & Black, Red Missale I, 1514* (22), and *Jam Jars in a Window. Pink & Turquoise* (13), with us both sitting looking at the original works. I performed all of them on the bassoon, my principal instrument, and Samuel performed on an arrangement of cymbals and an amplified wire. Ever since I first picked up the bassoon as a child I have been interested in the extreme contrast in sonorities between its pure high register and rasping, low sonorous register. Through the use of a range of extended techniques, including multiphonics, rhythmic key clicks and breathing out through the instrument, I was able to effectively blend the tonal palettes of the bassoon with Samuel's instruments so we were able to match the visual textural complexity of Janet's work with our musical material.

My PhD research was focussed around exploring the experience of performing musical graphics and this unique experience of playing in a studio where the original works were created provided me with a rare opportunity to analyse the levels of interpretive perspective that a performer goes through when engaging with musical graphics. There were specific details, such as the glass shelves and jam jars in the studio window reverberating whilst we played along with sounds from the garden, which merged with our music and influenced our interpretive responses.

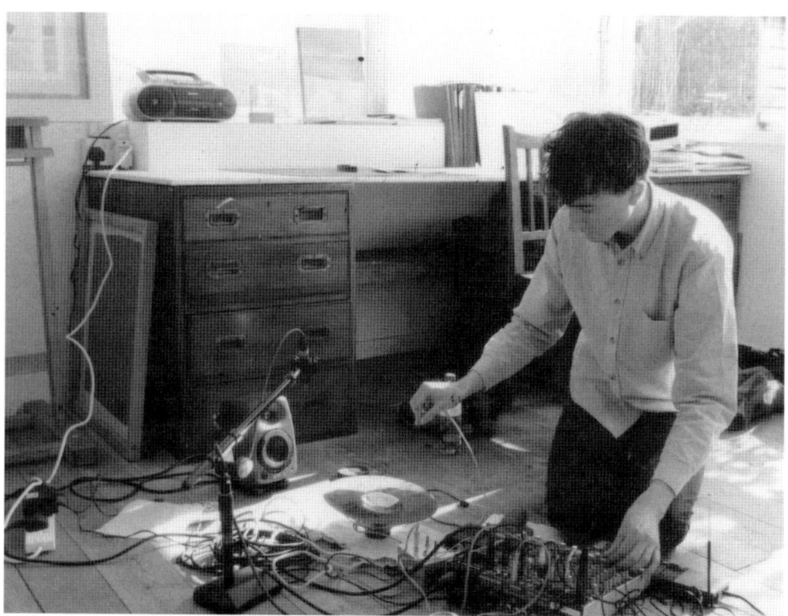

Simon Whalley
The Music Department, Keble College, Oxford; May 2014

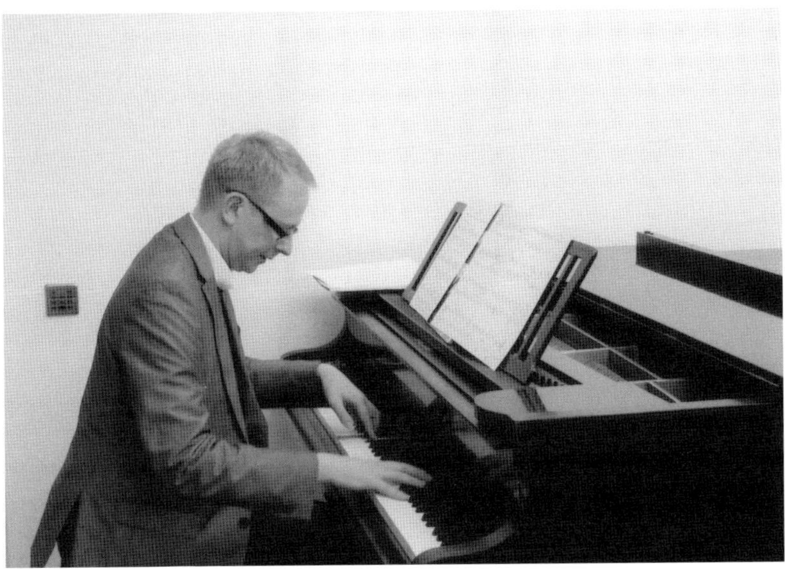

Chapel Recital and Compline

Jam Jars in a Window, Green & Terracotta (14) introduces almost disquieting discrete black squares or rectangles as they mark their glassy, limpid and watery context. These black shapes are reminiscent of plainchant neumes and the overall effect brings to mind stained glass and resonant church buildings, with their own watery acoustical qualities. Musical dots demand specific pitches and rhythms, relating one to another through ordered time; in these watercolour collages the black presence is not specifying pitches, nor does it require the rhyming precision of musical notations. Yet the black shapes punctuate and dance.

In *Red Missale I, 1514* (22) the vivid, brilliant scarlet is everything. It's startling impact is both shocking and familiar: it invokes the rich red of Pentecost, with all its fiery allusions; the intensity engages the viewer, demanding attention and contemplation. Plainchant notation was mostly staves, clefs and neumes written on beige vellum, but in some manuscripts red signified titles or indicated the start of a new word of liturgical significance. Here the overriding and overpowering redness suggests an opulent world of meaning and importance; the unutterable impact of the spirit moves through the strongly articulated verticals realised all the more powerfully through the sculpted

qualities of paperpulp relief. The use of plainchant compelled its
inclusion in the musical responses. The recital opened and closed with
Tudor motets that set a monodic hymn, including *Te Lucis* by Thomas
Tallis.

The Wardens's Recital

For this recital I also wrote and performed *Veni*, a piano work
responding to Janet's art. A well-known plainchant theme appropriate
for the Pentecost season—*veni creator spiritu*—is used as a 'cantus
firmus' (fixed chant) underpinning the whole and played in the bass
throughout. These deep slow notes arise from the suggestion of
plainchant's spiritual power in *Red Missale I, 1514* (22). A luminescent
contrast with the low chant appears as an array of rich, widely spaced
chords, exploring combinations of keys with contrasting musical
colours. Shapes suggested in the main melody are reimagined and
projected in a higher register; the black dots of the plainchant find
their textural counterpoint in the complex musical spaces of harmony.

Tom Soper

The Milton Gallery, St Paul's School, London; October 2015

Our music students tend to use DAWs (Digital Audio Workstations), which display to the composer a particular view of music in the making: coloured blocks of tracks, black lines of MIDI data, wave-form images of vocal and instrumental recordings. Joining with Janet to write for her 'Eye Music' series of paintings was a challenge for two of our final-year students, who were engaging with the score and its symbology like Egyptologists, faced with a variant hieroglyph found on a tomb wall.

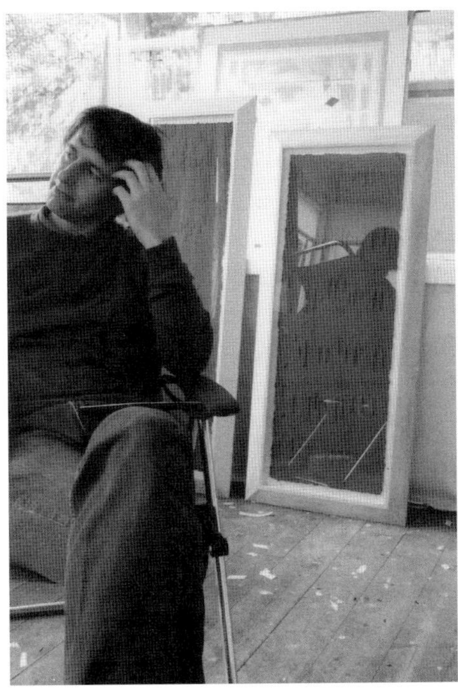

How to read it and how to write about it? They were attracted to the idea of composing to a more abstract brief than commercial composers tend to and their choice to 'write in' improvisation during the performance in the Milton Gallery Exhibition at St Pauls School worked a treat.

Although the market for composition of music, sound design and jingle has been in a state of upheaval, student composers are often keen to learn techniques and approaches that the current market seems to reward—perhaps to produce a thirty-second battle scene (for game or film) or a Thomas Newman-esque string arrangement. This commission was by comparison unconventional, it required deeper thinking and experimentation for which there was much less of a rule book. The 2020s will continue to see AI revolutionise the compositional process—"assisting the Lennon that needs a McCartney" as Spotify's Francois Pachet has put it. A project like this can encourage young artists to be less in awe of current conventions and more in awe of their own potential to find a way. 'Eye Music' unmoored them from dry territory and the experience was very beneficial.

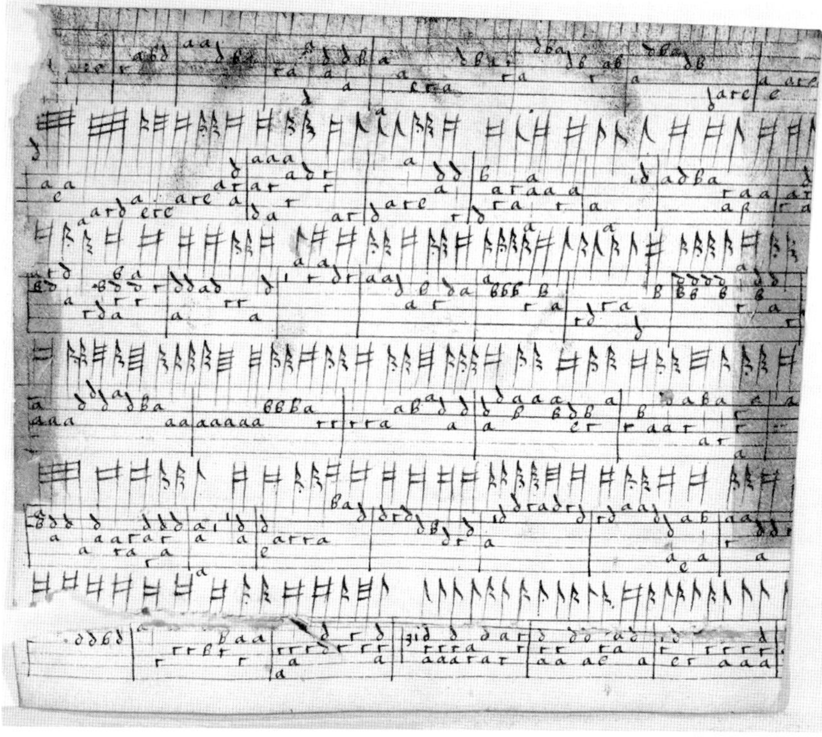

Fragments of lute tablature, probably English, c.1590-1600
(The Old Library, Magdalen College, Oxford)

Jonathan Arnold

Magdalen College, Oxford; October 2016

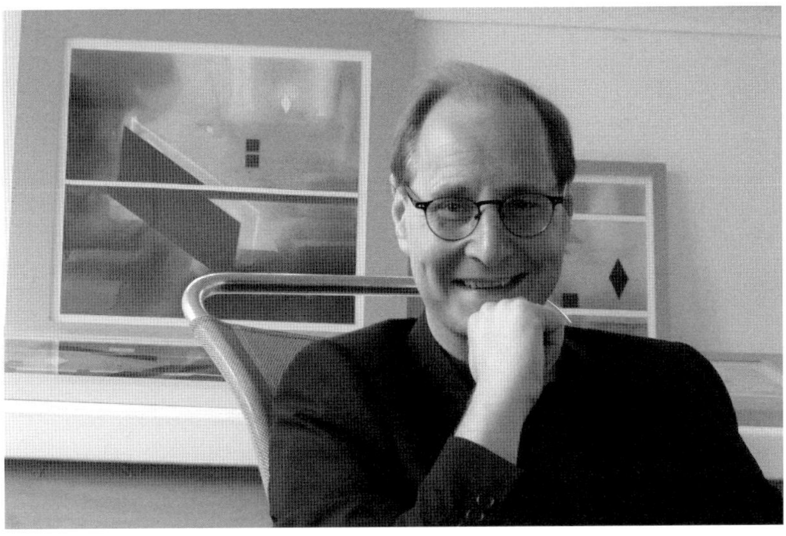

Walking through Janet's garden, I saw a depiction in slate and stone of the word "Faith" and further on Epicurus's injunction to "Live Unknown" cut into a piece of cherrywood. Both were placed in the borders beside the path leading to her studio. I was alerted to how the inclusion of words and signs, sometimes of a religious or moral nature, is important in her art. In her studio I was intrigued by the use of medieval notation within her compositions. The artistic connection between the sung notes within the Christian liturgy, particularly in the service of Tenebrae in Holy Week, is explored in a personal way, recognising the movement, both within the liturgy and within the heart of the believer, from darkness to light, from despair to hope.

'Fragments of Note: the afterlives of medieval manuscripts', examined the numerous medieval manuscript fragments held at Magdalen, largely medieval books which have been dismantled in the early modern period and re-used as binding waste or covers. The main exhibition took a particular focus on fragments featuring musical notation which were complemented by a selection of contemporary watercolour, collage and paperpulp relief works by Janet. She talked about her first encounter with the musical notation of lute tablature and being struck by the way the tablature "looks the way it sounds". Her artistic response captures the essence of 'visual sound' and works in response to the liturgy of Blackfriars or Magdalen Chapel encapsulate the experience of light, darkness, movement and sound.

For the final version of *Music and Faith: Conversations in a Post-Secular Age* (Boydell, 2018) we included her artwork on the covers, and at the beginning of each chapter colour plates of her works, from the early 'Eye Music' studies of jam jars, to artistic reflections on Tenebrae, plainchant, the Virgin and Child, lute music, as well as paintings inspired by the services, music and architecture of Magdalen College Chapel.

This connection between music and faith is not fanciful or romantic, but practical and grounded. Janet's theological perspective is rooted in realized eschatalogical notions that God is to be found in the here and now, with little regard for a future paradise. Joy, if it is to be found, is in the present moment. There is great joy to be found in the creativity within the inter-relationship between art of music, the movement and sound of the liturgy, which sweep through the time and space of the architectural tones of the chapel, and the faith of the participants and listeners. The mixture of manuscript notation, penned by anonymous monastics long ago, sung by clerics and clerks in churches and chapels as part of devotional worship and modern-day art works, link centuries of traditions in Western Christianity, including artists, musicians, theologians and priests and bring them together in the life of one human being and her response of faith.

Giovanni Varelli
Early Medieval Palimpsest Manuscripts

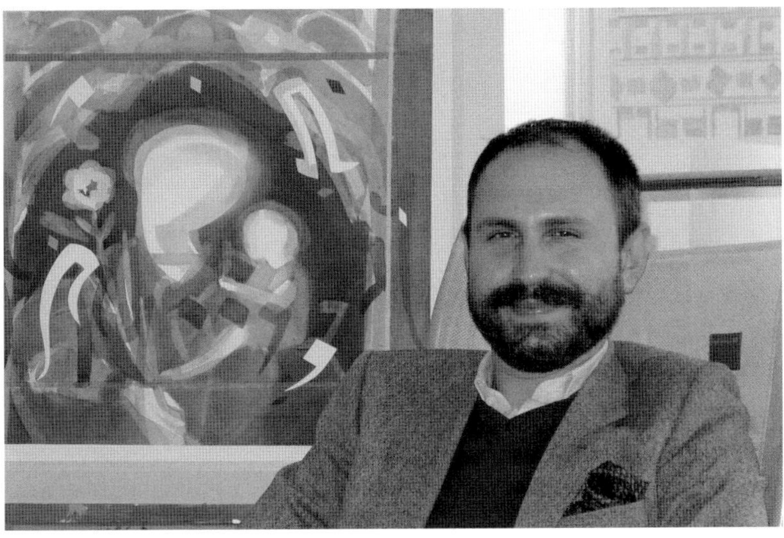

Knowledge is never whole, the way our minds interact with reality is through impressions formed of fragments. Art is an exceptional vehicle for recalling, relating and representing such fragments.

'Fragments of Note' displayed fragments of medieval music manuscripts from college collections, most discovered from inside bindings of early printed books, where they were re-used because of the durable quality of the parchment. Fragments (re)creating matter; fragments (re)constructing meaning. The collaboration with Janet Boulton aimed at achieving exactly such a relationship, that between impressions and artistic reactions.

One type of musical notation is particularly evocative in this respect: neumatic notation. Early liturgical chant began to be recorded in manuscripts in the ninth century, using graphic signs (neumes) that represented mostly the shape of the melody and some of its attributes, i.e. ascending, descending, lengthening, repeating, softening, etc. Little or no information was given to elements that we now consider eassential, like pitch and rhythm. In other words, neumatic notation was a system that only functioned within the limits of pre-established musical conventions: that is when the music could only be read when the singer already knew the melody mostly by heart. Neumes acted therefore as a support for memory, providing indications about its performance as well as fixing its contours. It was not until the late-eleventh century when neumes started to be written on a system of parallel lines that we now call 'staff', allowing singers to learn a new melody simply by reading it.

For centuries liturgical chant was seen through the mediation of these graphic shapes. Fragments of music manuscript that survive today allow us to look at written music through the same lenses as medieval singers (only we do not have their 'eyes'), just like light filters through a stained glass window. Janet Boulton masterfully captured this ethereal and aural dimension in her work, and most vividly in her *Neumes: Virgin & Child II* (37). The musical shapes in the piece are twelfth-century neumes, specifically of a Norman variety, although the manuscript in which they are contained was most likely written in south England, possibly Canterbury. Before the development of the staff, neumes were placed more freely on the manuscript page: the lack of boundaries, the appearance as if suspended, floating in the spatiality of a College chapel, is refined and paralleled in the features of the Virgin and Child.

Daryl Green
Fragments of Note: the afterlives of medieval manuscripts

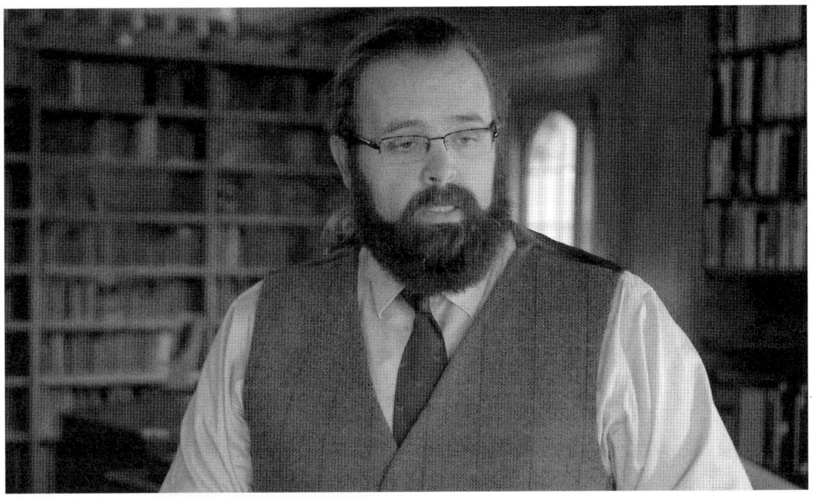

We met in the Old Library at Magdalen College, a large room on the
first floor above the cloisters, its bookshelves forming cosy alcoves in
front of the windows. In one of these Janet, Giovanni Varelli and myself
soon found ourselves poring over fragments of medieval manuscripts,
as well as complete manuscripts and early printed books containing
musical notation. Janet has a well-established interest in musical
notation and the space in which music lives: the emotions which art
and music and space evoke. Giovanni was like an overflowing spring of
information, jumping from neumes to staves and describing not only
how these manuscripts would have been produced but how they were
performed and why they were now in a fragmentary state. It was a
moment when the nature of our exhibition changed.

It became not only a show of musical fragments and book history,
but also a response to these things, from someone who did not have
the same background as myself, or Giovanni, or Jonathan Arnold: what
they see, what emotions these objects and historical artefacts evoke.

The exhibition became two parts that formed one; as you walked up
the long hall of the Old Library towards the historic exhibition, you
were greeted by Janet's painting, her reactions to that which was to
come, setting the tone for the viewer, for what they were about to see
in the physical artefacts. The paintings evoked emotion, they played
with light and shadow, they grounded the exhibition in a sense of
place and sense of attitude.

Lynda Sayce

Summer Common Room, Magdalen College, Oxford; January 2018

I was commissioned to transcribe the contents of two incomplete leaves containing sixteenth century lute tablature and to play a little music for a seminar accompanying 'Fragments of Note'. My involvement with Janet's work came about, almost accidentally, a spur of the moment interjection when a member of the audience invited me to play to the tablature symbols from her painting.

Magdalen's fragments punched far above their weight, their beauty, antiquity and often colourful history (recycled as endpapers or wrappers, or rescued from bindings) captivating the viewers. Some had exquisite decoration, made poignant by their fragmentary state—a single perfectly gilded initial, or a cascade of cobalt tendrils around a calligraphic letter. While it is hard not to feel sadness for the lost book, Janet's paintings prove oddly comforting: they effectively echoed and continued the music of the fragments. Janet places the musical notes sparingly in backgrounds of gently luminous colour, sometimes intersecting with bold angular lines. These lines and colours bringing to mind ecclesiastical architecture and the pools of coloured light created by stained glass, but the paintings also create a church-like ambience in the viewer's mind, into which the notes drift as focussed and powerful as plainsong in the reverberance of a cathedral. The

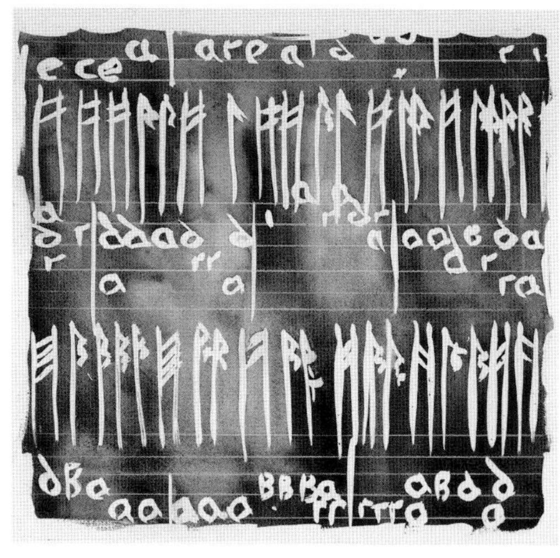

Lute Tablature: Cloister I (night), watercolour, 2017

painted notes are few, and surrounded as they are by light and shade, they hint at something larger, as do the fragments; I was reminded of Shakespeare's "Bare ruined choirs, where late the sweet birds sang".

In this reverential atmosphere, the lute tablature fragments seemed plebeian scraps, crowded with tiny cyphers of gnarly intricacy, their notation alien to most viewers. These paper leaves sat humbly alongside the sumptuous remains of parchment treasures, their connection to an instrument so associated with domestic music making them appear as out of place as a banjo in a monastic choir. Janet's tablature painting also stood out arresting in its boldness, a chilly colour palette and a lot of black, slashed with gleaming bone-white ciphers, busily cursive, seemingly angry—or at least argumentative. Letters—which tell the lutenist where to stop the strings—were strewn across the painting,

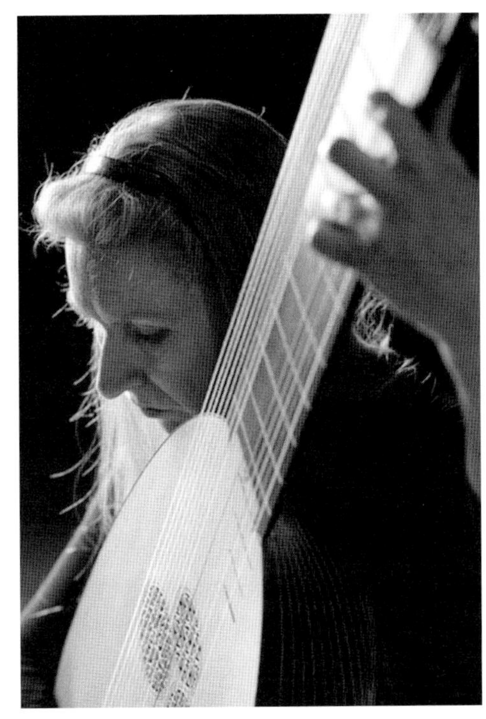

clamouring for attention, demanding to be read, but always denying the viewer the satisfaction of comprehension. Tablature letters only rarely make words, so are always Babelesque.

Though both of our contributions were closely connected to the manuscript fragments, our expected audiences—lovers of contemporary painting and enthusiasts of renaissance lute music—tend, in my experience, to be mutually exclusive groups. In the end my enduring memory of the event was the joyful enthusiasm with which the two groups embraced each others' interests.

James Crockford

Magdalen College Chapel, Oxford; June 2019

Three works *Tenebrae II*; *Lamentations*; *Stabat Mater*—were to be the focus of a musical reading, a sound experience, as part of a day's symposium on 'Music, Art and Faith' in June 2019. Without yet knowing how, I would be improvising live interpretations on the soprano saxophone, with a group of plainchant singers at Magdalen College Chapel.

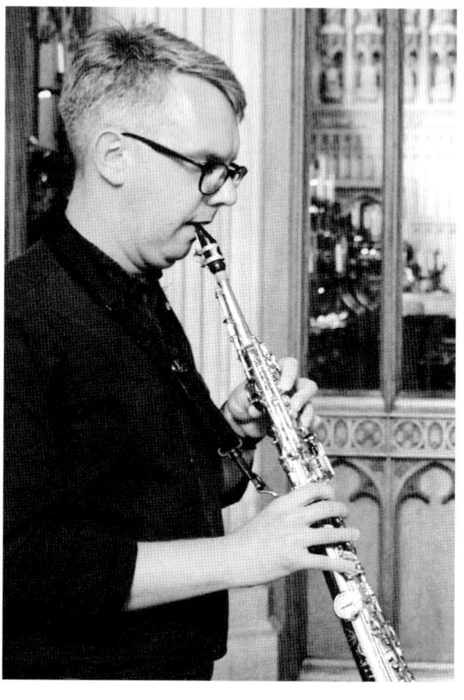

The final response to the *Stabat Mater* (30) I performed solo, standing in the midst of the viewers, all facing the work together. One of the most remarkable effects of the experience was the way in which the sound response sets up a sort of immersion of the performer (and perhaps the listener also) in the art's own living presence. I found myself playing from within the art, reading and voicing it, exploring its significances and suggestions as I looked, bringing them to birth in sound. You can't 'play' a piece of art, and certainly not all in one note—I was committed to a journey, to telling a story. But because you are improvising it is a very living, breathing story, one you only find as you move through it.

As I looked and played, how did I do that translation, if that's even the word? Perhaps a re-experiencing, an offering are better terms. I found there were not thoughts that linked my seeing and my playing directly, but a very immediate level of interpretive connections running through the mind and the body. Just as we rarely process our speaking, or moving our limbs to walk, I let myself be carried along by the ways in which my seeing connected with and generated the expressions of sound that my hands, throat and mouth, knew how to make intuitively.

I had the vaguest ideas about how I might enter into the improvisation. There's one large lozenge note in the picture that leans down, and I heard this as a falling groan of pain—the pain of Christ in anguish, the pain of Mary who is told that "a sword will pierce your own soul too". I found myself making use of a range of sound techniques that sit somewhere between silence and noise, in that half-way space of groans and breaths and growls and distortion of harmonics. These gutteral and vulnerable effects were an evocative and powerful expression of the pain and violence, the wrenching, that I perceived as I looked. In the immediacy of the improvisation, the climax came in a shooting, piercing high note shrieking out, only to die away. The meditation (this might be the best word for it) ended as sound died away slowly to just a breath moving through the saxophone—as if Christ, the shrieks of anguish dying away, finally breathes his last and gives up his spirit. Then, the thickest silence.

When the soprano saxophone of the Rev. James Crockford was heard soaring above our plainchant as he improvised his response to the image before him, it was an electrifying moment where voice, instrument, sound and image, acoustic, light and crafted stone combined in a multi-sensory encounter with the sublime. Our job as singers was to be faithful to the discipline of the plainchant, which has been for centuries the heartbeat of the monastic and religious tradition of the church. Finding the singers was of course no difficulty, for I had some of the 'Academical Clerks' or Gentlemen of the Chapel Choir to hand. But as James' inspired melodies and rhythms played and danced above us and around us, we had also to acknowledge and respond to the ornamentation of the lyrical sax surrounding us.

—Jonathan Arnold

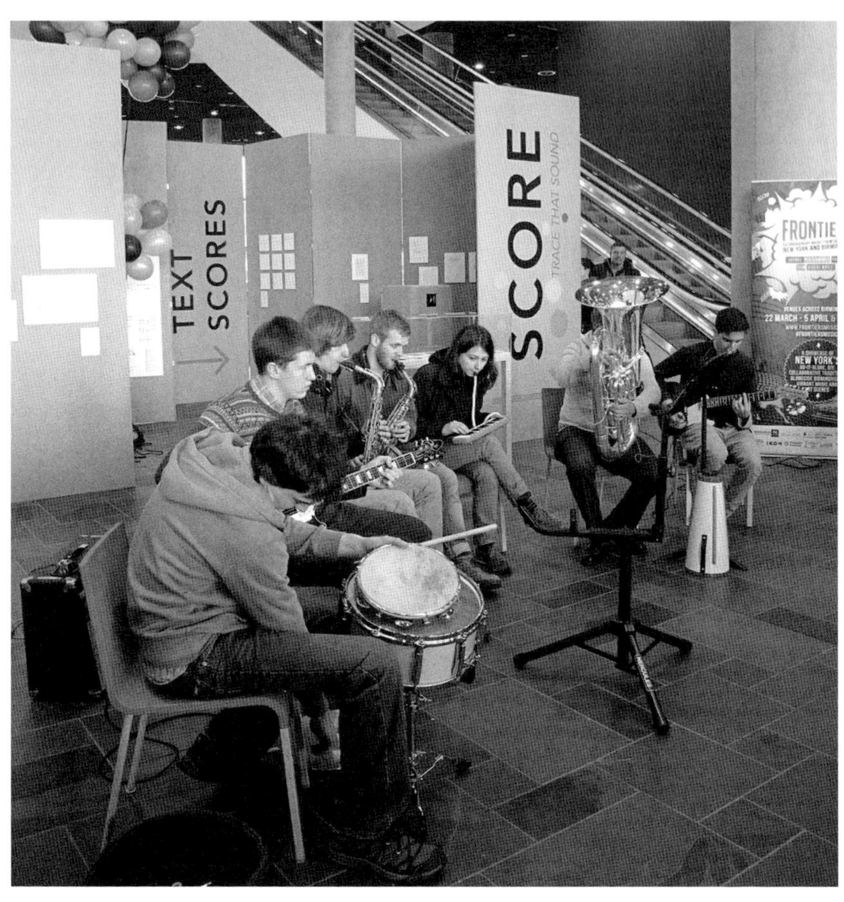

Performers at The Library of Birmingham, 2014

Events

The 'Frontiers Festival' of experimental music held in March and April 2014 at the then newly-opened Library of Birmingham, included participation in a seminar chaired by Joe Scarffe, with Adam De La Cour, Carl Bergstrøm-Nielsen and Andrew Ingamells at the library, and the workshop 'Deep Listening' with Pauline Oliveras at Ikon Gallery. A series of concerts concluded with a septet performance of *Jam Jars in a Window, Grey & Black* consisting soprano voice, bowed cymbals and live electronics, bassoon, clarinet, saxophone and trumpet. It was recorded for a special festival broadcast of 'Here and Now' for BBC Radio 3, which also included a discussion of the exhibition of graphic scores 'Score: Trace that Sound', curated by Joe Scarffe.

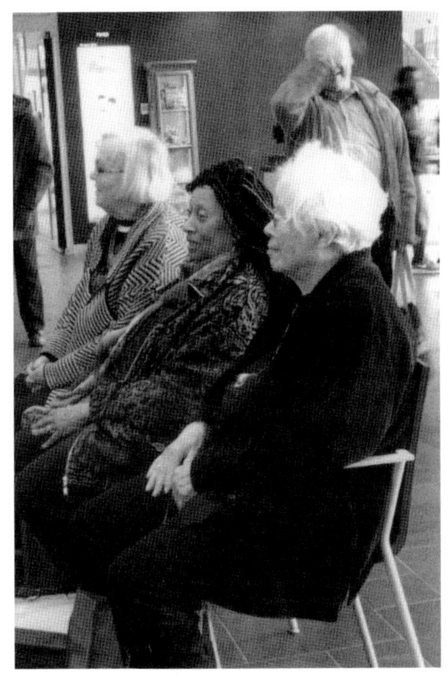

Janet Boulton, Ione, Pauline Oliveras

In May 2014 an exhibition of 'Eye Music' paintings and paper relief works was held at Keble College Oxford, with two piano recitals by Simon Whalley in the Music Department of the College on the 22nd and 23rd, responding to the works *Jam Jars in a Window, Green & Terracotta* and *Red Missale, 1514*.

An exhibition of 'Eye Music' works was held at The Milton Gallery, St Paul's School, London from 24 September to 15 October 2015. A workshop was directed by Tom Soper, course leader of the Faculty of Media, Arts and Technology, University of Gloucestershire, with performances responding to the images by final-year students Ollie Weikert and Eli Nicklin.

'Fragments of Note: the afterlives of medieval manuscripts' an exhibition from the collection curated by Giovanni Varelli and Daryl Green, was held in The Old Library, Magdalen College, and ran from 23 November 2017 to 19 April 2018. On 22 January there was a presentation and performance in the Summer Common Room, with a conversation between Jonathan Arnold, Daryl Green and Janet Boulton, and a recital of manuscript fragments from the Magdalen collection and the artist's *Lute Tablatures* by the lutenist Lynda Sayce.

The symposium 'Conversations in Music, Art and Faith', with Jonathan Arnold at Magdalen College Chapel, Oxford on 15 June 2019, was held to coincide with the publication of his book *Music and Faith: Conversations in a Post-Secular Age*. It included a conversation between the author and Janet Boulton about 'Eye Music', and musical responses to her 'Three Studies for Holy Week' performed by James Crockford playing soprano saxophone, and singers Jonathan Arnold, Chris Murphy and Richard Douglas.

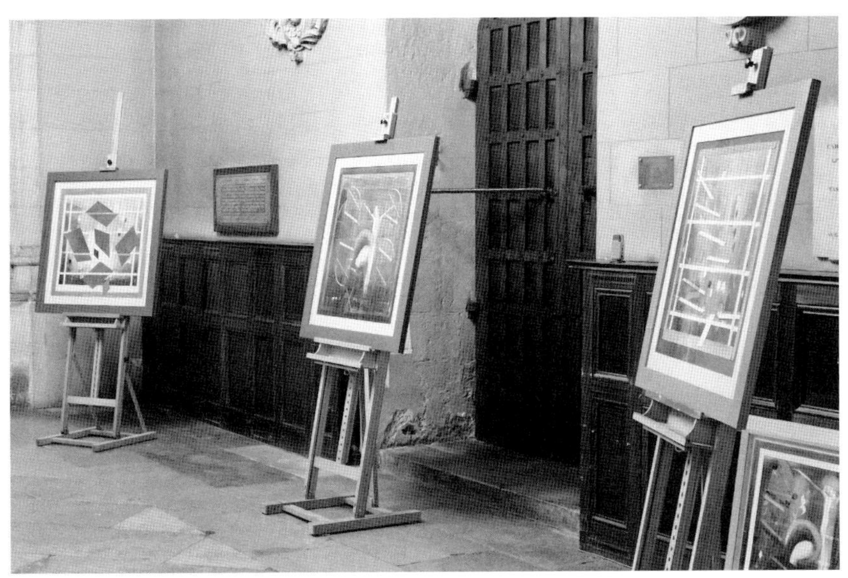

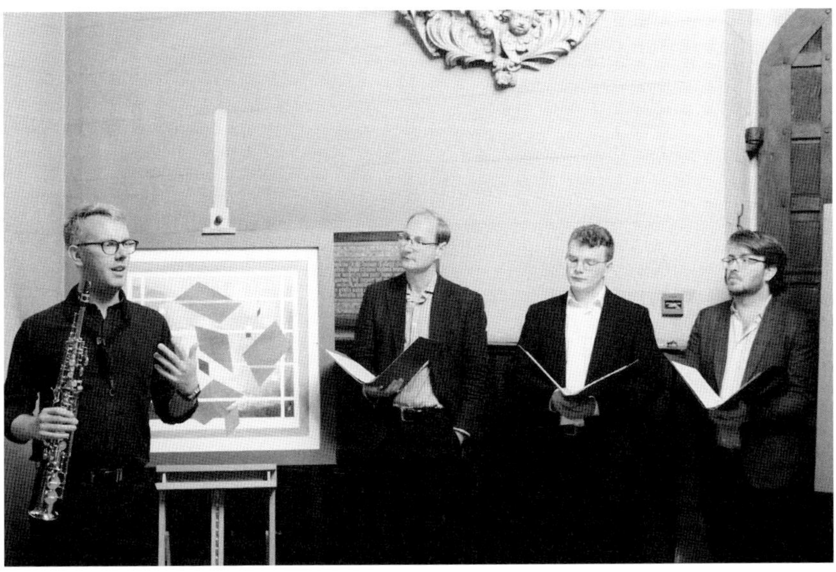

'Three Studies for Holy Week', Magdalen College Chapel, Oxford, 2019

Writers

Rev. Dr Jonathan Arnold was a professional singer before being ordained, and made numerous recordings with The Sixteen, Polyphony, the Tallis Singers and others. Recent publications include *Music and Faith: Conversations in a Post-Secular Age* (2019) and *Sacred Music in Secular Society* (2014). Currently he is Director of Communities and Partnerships in the Diocese of Canterbury.

Rev. Dr James Crockford is Dean of Chapel, Tutor and Fellow at Jesus College Cambridge. Prior to ordination he read music at the University of Nottingham and holds a fellowship of the Royal School of Music in saxophone performance. Alongside his pastoral duties, he researches and writes on the intersection of music and theology, with particular interest in textual and hermeneutical theory.

Daryl Green FSA is a librarian, bibliographer, and researcher. He has worked with manuscripts and early printed books for over a decade at York Minster Library, The University of Illinois Urbana-Champaign, the University of St Andrews and as Head Librarian at Magdalen College, Oxford. Currently he is Head of Special Collections and Deputy Head of Centre for Research Collections, University of Edinburgh.

Lynda Sayce is one of Britains foremost lutenists, and known also as a scholar of musical history of the lute and theorbo. Widely recorded, she performs regularly as a soloist and continuo player with leading instrumental ensembles worldwide, and is principal lutenist with La Serenissima, The Kings Consort and Ex Cathedra.

Dr Joe Scarffe is a researcher who specialises in performing graphic scores and is an editor for International Improvised Music Archive. He is also Head of Marketing at Global Creative Marketplace. He lives and farms in Wiltshire.

Tom Soper is Course Leader in Popular Music at the Faculty of Media, Arts and Technology, University of Gloucestershire.

Dr Giovanni Varelli is Prize Fellow in Music at Magdalen College Oxford. His research interests span Latin paleaography and codicology, medieval liturgy, music theory and notation, philology and reception history, manuscripts' digital restoration and conservation. He is currently a Fellow of Villa I Tatti, Harvard University Center of Italian Renaissance Studies, Florence.

Simon Whalley is a freelance composer and choral conductor. Following a long period as Fellow and Director of Music at Keble College, Oxford, he now focuses mainly on his own work and is currently composing a work for counter tenor and string orchestra based on texts by the metaphysical poets.